JN319937

NOTES
ON
HOSPITALS

BY
FLORENCE NIGHTINGALE

Third Edition
1863

＜復刻版＞

I dedicate this reprinting to H. Arai, RN, who received the Order of the Sacred Treasure, Silver Rays in November 2005, S. Miyake, RN, who was appointed Professor of Nursing in April 2006, and S. Sakamoto, RN, who was appointed Professor of Nursing in April 2006.

Reprinted 2006 by
SAIWAISHOBO Co. Ltd.
3-17, Jinbo-cho, Kanda,
Chiyoda-ku, Tokyo, JAPAN, 101-0051

To

Sir William G. Armstrong
Kt. CB. FRS

with the complements of the
Committee of the "Nightingale Fund"

30 April / 70.

Prof. Hiroyoshi Kobayashi MD PhD
23 January. 2006

NOTES

ON

HOSPITALS.

BY

FLORENCE NIGHTINGALE

Third Edition,

Enlarged and for the most part Re-written.

LONDON:
LONGMAN, GREEN, LONGMAN, ROBERTS, AND GREEN.
1863.

LONDON:

SAVILL AND EDWARDS, PRINTERS, CHANDOS-STREET,

COVENT-GARDEN.

PREFACE.

It may seem a strange principle to enunciate as the very first requirement in a Hospital that it should do the sick no harm. It is quite necessary, nevertheless, to lay down such a principle, because the actual mortality *in* hospitals, especially in those of large crowded cities, is very much higher than any calculation founded on the mortality of the same class of diseases among patients treated *out of* hospital would lead us to expect. The knowledge of this fact first induced me to examine into the influence exercised by hospital construction on the duration and death-rate of cases received into the wards; and it led me to lay before the Social Science Association a paper reprinted with the present title. Since the publication of the first edition of that paper, great advances have been made in the adoption of sound principles of hospital construction; and there are already a number of examples of new hospitals realizing all, or nearly all, the conditions required for the successful treatment of the sick and maimed poor. Besides this, much additional experience has been obtained in many important points, especially in the details of hospital buildings and fittings.

In order to spread a knowledge of the progress already made, as well as of those principles which may now be considered as established, I have been asked to prepare the present edition. In doing this, it has been necessary to re-write nearly the whole of it, and to make so many additions to the matter that it is in reality a new book.

F. N.

INDEX TO SUBJECTS.

APPENDIX.

LIST OF PLANS.

THE PLANS OF LONDON AND PARIS TO BE INSERTED AT THE END.

NOTES ON HOSPITALS.

IT is proposed in the following pages to give—1st, a general account of the sanitary condition of existing hospitals; 2nd, a statement of those structural defects in hospitals which have influenced the progress of medical and surgical cases while under treatment in them; 3rd, the principles of construction which ought to be kept in view in building new hospitals; 4th, improved plans for hospitals and convalescent-institutions;—and lastly, certain proposals adopted by the International Statistical Congress for improving the method of tabulating hospital statistics, together with a proposal for an uniform system of registering statistics of surgical operations, their complications and results.

I. SANITARY CONDITION OF HOSPITALS.

No one, I think, who brings ordinary powers of observation to bear on the sick and maimed, can fail to observe a remarkable difference in the aspect of cases, in their duration and in their termination in different hospitals. To the superficial observer there are two things only apparent—the disease and the remedial treatment, medical or surgical. It requires a considerable amount of experience, in hospitals of various constructions and varied administrations, to go beyond this, and to be able to perceive that conditions arising out of these elements have a very powerful effect indeed upon the ultimate issue of cases which pass through the wards.

It is sometimes asserted that there is no such striking difference in the mortality of different hospitals as one would be led to infer from their great apparent difference in sanitary condition. There is, undoubtedly, some difficulty in arriving at correct statistical comparison to exhibit this. For, in the first place, different hospitals receive very different proportions of the same class of diseases. The ages in one hospital may differ considerably from the ages in another. And the state of the cases on admission may differ very much in each hospital. These elements affect considerably the results of treatment, altogether apart from the sanitary state of hospitals. But the fact has sometimes been made use of in a way no one could have anticipated. A high and increasing death rate has been actually put forward, not as the result of these causes, but as the result of increasing celebrity; which can have no other practical meaning than this:—that a greater number of people go there to die next year, because so many have died there this year; a principle equally applicable in private practice, and according to which, the physician or surgeon who loses the largest percentage of cases is the man most worthy of confidence.

In the next place, accurate hospital statistics are much more rare than is generally imagined, and at the best they only give the mortality which has taken place *in* the hospitals, and take no cognizance of those cases which are discharged in a hopeless condition, to die immediately afterwards, a practice which is followed to a much greater extent by some hospitals than by others.

We have known incurable cases discharged from one hospital, to which the deaths ought to have been accounted, and received into another hospital, to die there in a day or two after admission, thereby lowering the mortality rate of the first at the expense of the second.

Making every allowance for difficulties attending an inquiry into the comparative mortality of hospitals, there are nevertheless certain very startling facts, which ought to arrest the attention of every one interested in the welfare of sick or maimed. The Registrar-General, in his last Annual Report, has given a set of Occasional Tables on the Mortality of Public Institutions in England, which contain data of more than usual interest and importance on this subject. Returns were obtained from 106 hospitals, giving the number of inmates in each hospital on April 8th, 1861. This number is taken as an approximation to the average of inmates at each establishment. The number of deaths registered in each hospital during the year 1861 is also given—so that, assuming the approximate accuracy of the data, the mortality per cent. in each hospital can be ascertained for the year. The following classified abstract contains the results of the inquiry, and they are certainly striking enough:—

Mortality per Cent. in the principal Hospitals of England. 1861.

—	Number of Special Inmates on the 8th April, 1861.	Average Number of Inmates in each Hospital.	Number of Deaths registered in the Year 1861.	Mortality per Cent. on Inmates.
In 106 Principal Hospitals of England	12709	120	7227	56·87
24 London Hospitals	4214	176	3828	90·84
12 Hospitals in Large Towns ...	1870	156	1555	83·16
25 County and Important Provincial Hospitals	2248	90	886	39·41
30 Other Hospitals	1136	38	457	40·23
13 Naval and Military Hospitals ...	3000	231	470	15·67
1 Royal Sea Bathing Infirmary (Margate)	133	133	17	12·78
1 Dane Hill Metropolitan Infirmary (Margate)	108	108	14	12·96

It will be seen that the hospitals are grouped according to locality. Now let us compare three of these groups with each other. We have 24 London hospitals, affording a mortality of no less than 90·84 per cent., very nearly every bed yielding a death in the course of the year. Next, we have 12 hospitals in large provincial towns, Bristol, Birmingham, Liverpool, Manchester, &c., yielding a death rate of 83·16 per cent. And there are 25 county hospitals in country towns, the mortality in which is no more than 39·41 per cent. Here we have at once a hospital problem demanding solution. However the great differences in the death rates may be explained, it cannot be denied that the most unhealthy hospitals are those situated within the vast circuit of the metropolis; that the next lower death rate takes place in hospitals in densely populated large manufacturing and commercial towns, and that by far the most healthy hospitals are those of the smaller country towns.

These results are quite reliable, and are preferable to those derived from individual hospitals. Otherwise, it might be stated that the death rate of certain hospitals situated in large towns is so enormous that every bed is cleared out in the year, and in some of them once in about 9 months.

Facts such as these (and it is not the first time that they have been placed before the public) have sometimes raised grave doubts as to the advantages to be derived from hospitals at all, and have led many an one to think that in all probability a poor sufferer would have a much better chance of recovery if treated at home.

The sanitary state of any hospital ought not, however, to be inferred solely from the greater or less mortality. If the function of a hospital were to kill the sick, statistical comparisons of this nature would be admissible. As, however, its proper function is to restore the sick to health as speedily as possible, the elements which really give information as to whether this is done or not, are those which show the proportion of sick restored to health, and the average time which has been required for this object; a hospital which restored all its sick to health after an average of six months' treatment, could not be considered as by any means so healthy as a hospital which returned all its sick recovered in as many weeks. The proportion of recoveries, the proportion of deaths, and the average time in hospital, must all be taken into account in discussions of this nature, as well as the character of the cases and the proportion of different ages among the sick; and this brings me to the great importance of correct hospital statistics as an essential element in hospital administration.

Hospital mortality statistics have hitherto given little information on the efficiency of the hospital, *i. e.*, as to the extent to which it fulfils the purpose it was established for, because there are elements in existence of which such statistics have hitherto taken no cognizance. In one set of hospitals, in the table, I find the mortality from 12½ to 15½ per cent. upon the cases treated, while in other hospitals the deaths reach from 83 to 90½ per cent. To judge by the mortality only in these cases would be most fallacious. Because in the first class of hospitals ailments not of a dangerous nature constitute a title to hospital admission, while, in the latter class of hospitals, dangerous and special diseases, at all times accompanied by a high rate of mortality, are largely admitted. Hence the duration of the cases admitted, and the general course and aspect of disease, afford important criteria whereby to judge of the healthiness or unhealthiness of any hospital, in addition to that afforded by the mortality statistics.

Perhaps the most delicate test of anitary condition in

hospitals is afforded by the progress and termination of surgical cases after operation, together with the complications which they present. The statistics of medical cases, although affording important data for our purpose, are of themselves imperfect indices of the healthiness of wards, but it is otherwise with operation cases. In these the constitution gives immediate evidence of suffering from the neglect of hygiene, and many a life is sacrificed from not recognising this fact. In another section I have dealt with this important subject, and have given the method of keeping the Statistics of Hospitals proposed by me, and adopted by the International Statistical Congress; and also a proposal for registering surgical operations and their results.

Careful observers are now generally convinced that the origin and spread of fever in a hospital, or the appearance and spread of hospital gangrene, erysipelas, and pyæmia generally, are much better tests of the defective sanitary state of a hospital than its mortality returns.* But I would go further, and state that to the experienced eye of a careful observing nurse, the daily, I had almost said hourly, changes which take place in patients, and which changes rarely come under the cognizance of the periodical medical visitor, afford a still more

* The following suggestive passages from Mr. Paget's address, delivered before the British Medical Association, 1862, have an important bearing on this subject:

"In every case of erysipelas, pyæmia, or the like, we ought to work till we can discover its probable origin; we should have the strongest feeling that these diseases are not spontaneous nor inevitable. In every case, the hospital, or the house, or our own practice, should be brought to trial—to private trial, if you will, yet a just and true trial—a trial before our own conscience; and if the hospital, the house, or the practice be found guilty, let it be condemned and amended."

"Of all the remedies I have used or seen in use, I can find but one thing that I can call remedial for the whole disease, pyæmia: and that is a profuse supply of fresh air. In the three most remarkable recoveries I have seen, the patients might be said to have lain day and night in the wind—wind blowing all about their rooms."

important class of data, from which to judge of the general adaptation of a hospital for the reception and treatment of sick. One insensibly allies together restlessness, languor, feverishness, and general *malaise*, with closeness of wards, defective ventilation, defective structure, bad architectural and administrative arrangements, until it is impossible to resist the conviction that the sick are suffering from something quite other than the disease inscribed on their bed-ticket—and the inquiry insensibly arises in the mind, what can be the cause? To this query many years' experience of hospitals in various countries and climates enables me to answer explicitly as the result of my own observation, that, even admitting to the full extent the great value of the hospital improvements of recent years, a vast deal of the suffering, and some at least of the mortality, in these establishments is avoidable.

What, then, are those defects to which such results are to be attributed?

I should state at once that to original defects in the sites and plans of hospitals, and to deficient ventilation and overcrowding accompanying such defects, is to be attributed a large proportion of the evil I have mentioned.

The facts flow almost of necessity from ascertained sanitary experience. But it is not often, excepting perhaps in the case of intelligent house-surgeons, that the whole process whereby the sick, who ought to have had rapid recoveries, are retained week after week, or perhaps month after month, in hospital, is continuously observed. I have known a case of slight fever received into hospital, the fever pass off in less than a week, and yet the patient, from the foul state of the wards, not restored to health at the end of eight weeks.

I appeal to all careful hospital officers whether each has not known, within his own experience, instances on a large and fatal scale of disease produced in hospital; I myself could fill a book with them. One such may be given. In a small hospital, in one of the healthiest counties in England, in nine months, twenty-four poor creatures ran the gauntlet of their lives from erysipelas alone, of which disease eight died; and most of these after very trifling accidents or operations. None of them ought to have produced erysipelas at all; much less have ended fatally.

But on the very threshold of the subject we shall probably be told that to 'contagion' and 'infection' is much of the unhealthy condition of some hospitals attributable, at least so far as concerns the occurrence of zymotic diseases. On the very threshold, therefore, we are obliged to make a digression, in order to discuss the meaning of these two familiar words, and to lay these spectres which have terrified almost all ages and nations.

This is the more necessary, because on the exact influence exercised by these two presumed causes of hospital sickness and mortality depends to a great degree the possibility of our introducing efficient hospital attendance and nursing. Unfortunately both nurses* and medical men, as well as medical students, have died of zymotic diseases prevailing in hospitals. It is an all-important question to decide whether the propagation of such diseases is inevitable or preventible. If the former, then the whole question must be considered as to whether hospitals necessarily attended with results so fatal should exist at all. If the latter, then it is our duty to prevent their propagation.

The idea of 'contagion,' as explaining the spread of disease, appears to have been adopted at a time when, from the neglect of sanitary arrangements, epidemics attacked whole masses of

* See Note A, at the end of this section.

people, and when men had ceased to consider that nature had any laws for her guidance. Beginning with the poets and historians, the word finally made its way into medical nomenclature,* where it has remained ever since, affording to certain classes of minds, chiefly in the southern and less educated parts of Europe, a satisfactory reason for pestilence, and an adequate excuse for non-exertion to prevent its recurrence.

And now, what does 'contagion' mean? It implies the communication of disease from person to person by *contact.* It pre-supposes the existence of certain germs like the sporules of fungi, which can be bottled up and conveyed any distance attached to clothing, to merchandize, especially to woollen stuffs, for which it is supposed to have a particular affection, and to feathers, which of all articles it especially loves—so much so, that, according to quarantine laws, a live goose may be safely introduced from a plague country; but if it happen to be eaten on the voyage, its feathers cannot be admitted without danger to the entire community. There is no end to the absurdities connected with this doctrine. Suffice it to say, that in the ordinary sense of the word, there is no proof, such as would be admitted in any scientific inquiry, that there is any such thing as 'contagion.'

There are two or three diseases in which there is a specific virus, which can be seen, tasted, smelt, and analysed, and which in certain constitutions propagates the original disease by inoculation—such as small-pox, cow-pox, &c. But these are not 'contagions' in the sense supposed.†

* See Note B, at the end of this section.

† Curiously enough, these directly communicable diseases were excluded from the operation of general quarantine law by the International Quarantine Conference of Paris, 1851, which restricted the objects of quarantine to plague, yellow fever, and cholera, while it gave a logical *coup de grace* to the 'contagion' hypothesis by abolishing the 'suspected bill of health.'

The word 'infection,' which is often confounded with 'contagion,' expresses a fact, and does not involve a hypothesis. But just as there is no such thing as 'contagion,' there is no such thing as *inevitable* 'infection.' Infection acts through the air. Poison the air breathed by individuals, and there is infection. Shut up 150 healthy people in a Black-hole of Calcutta, and in twenty-four hours an infection is produced so intense that it will, in that time, have destroyed nearly the whole of the inmates. Sick people are more susceptible than healthy people; and if they be shut up without sufficient space and sufficient fresh air, there will be produced not only fever, but erysipelas, pyæmia, and the usual tribe of hospital-generated epidemic diseases.

Again, if we have a fever hospital with over-crowded, badly-ventilated wards, we are quite certain to have the air become so infected as to poison the blood not only of the sick, so as to increase their mortality, but also of the medical attendants and nurses, so that they also shall become subjects of fever.

It will be seen at a glance, that in every such case and in every such example, the 'infection' is not inevitable, but simply the result of carelessness and ignorance. As soon as this practical view of the subject is admitted and acted upon, we shall cease to hear of hospital contagions.

In certain hospitals it has been the custom to set apart wards for what are called 'infectious' diseases, but in reality there ought to be no diseases so considered. With proper sanitary precautions, diseases reputed to be the most 'infectious' may be treated in wards among other sick without any danger. Without proper sanitary arrangements, a number of healthy people may be congregated together so as to become subject to the worst horrors of 'infection.'

No stronger condemnation of any hospital or ward could

be pronounced than the simple fact that any zymotic disease has originated in it, or that such diseases have attacked other patients than those brought in with them. And there can be no stronger condemnation of any town than the outbreak of fatal epidemics in it. Infection, and incapable management, or bad construction, are, in hospitals as well as in towns, convertible terms.

It was necessary to say thus much to show to what hospital diseases are *not* necessarily due. To the following defects in site, construction, and management, as we think, they are mainly to be attributed.

1. *The agglomeration of a large number of sick under one roof*

It is a well-established fact that, other things being equal, the amount of sickness and mortality on different areas bears a ratio to the degree of density of the population.

Why should undue agglomeration of sick be any exception to this law? Is it not rather to be expected that, the constitutions of sick people being more susceptible than those of healthy people, they should suffer more from this cause?

There is a reason, of course, for everything, and in the present case the reason why agglomeration of a large number of sick under one roof leads to disaster, is the simple fact, that agglomeration argues either stern necessities of another kind, or great ignorance and danger of mismanagement, and, besides all this, it argues unforeseen events, and altogether such a deficiency in the general administrative arrangements, as is sure to be accompanied by want of proper ventilation, want of cleanliness, and other sanitary defects.

If anything were wanting in confirmation of this fact, it would be the enormous mortality in the hospitals which contained perhaps the largest number of sick ever at one time under the same roof, viz., those at Scutari. The largest of these too famous hospitals had at one time 2500 sick and wounded under its roof, and it has happened that of Scutari patients two out of every five have died. In the hospital tents of the Crimea, although the sick were almost without shelter, without blankets, without proper food or medicines, the mortality was not above one-half what it was at Scutari; but these tents had only a few beds in each. Nor was it even so high as this in the small Balaclava General Hospital, which had part of its sick placed in detached wooden huts. While in the well-ventilated detached huts of the Castle Hospital, on the heights above Balaclava, exposed to the sea breeze, at a subsequent period, the mortality among the wounded did not reach three per cent. It is not to the comparative healthiness of these small hospitals, however, that we appeal, as the only proof of the danger of surface over-crowding. It is to the fact of 80 cases of hospital gangrene having been recorded during one month at Scutari (and many, many more passed unrecorded); to the fact that, out of 44 secondary amputations of the lower extremities consecutively performed, 36 have died; and to the cases of fever which broke out in the hospital, not by tens, but by hundreds.

But by far the most remarkable illustration of the effects produced on the sick and maimed by agglomeration, is that afforded by the experience of the Hôtel Dieu, at the latter end of the last century, and before its reconstruction.

I am indebted to M. Husson's "Etude sur les Hôpitaux" for a plan (No. 1) of the Hôtel Dieu, as it then was, showing the relation of all parts of the hospital on the same floor. It will be observed that there was direct atmospheric communication through the entire suite of wards occupied by above 550 beds on a single floor. The whole hospital contained 1200 beds. But the number of beds by no means represented the

Plan No. 1.

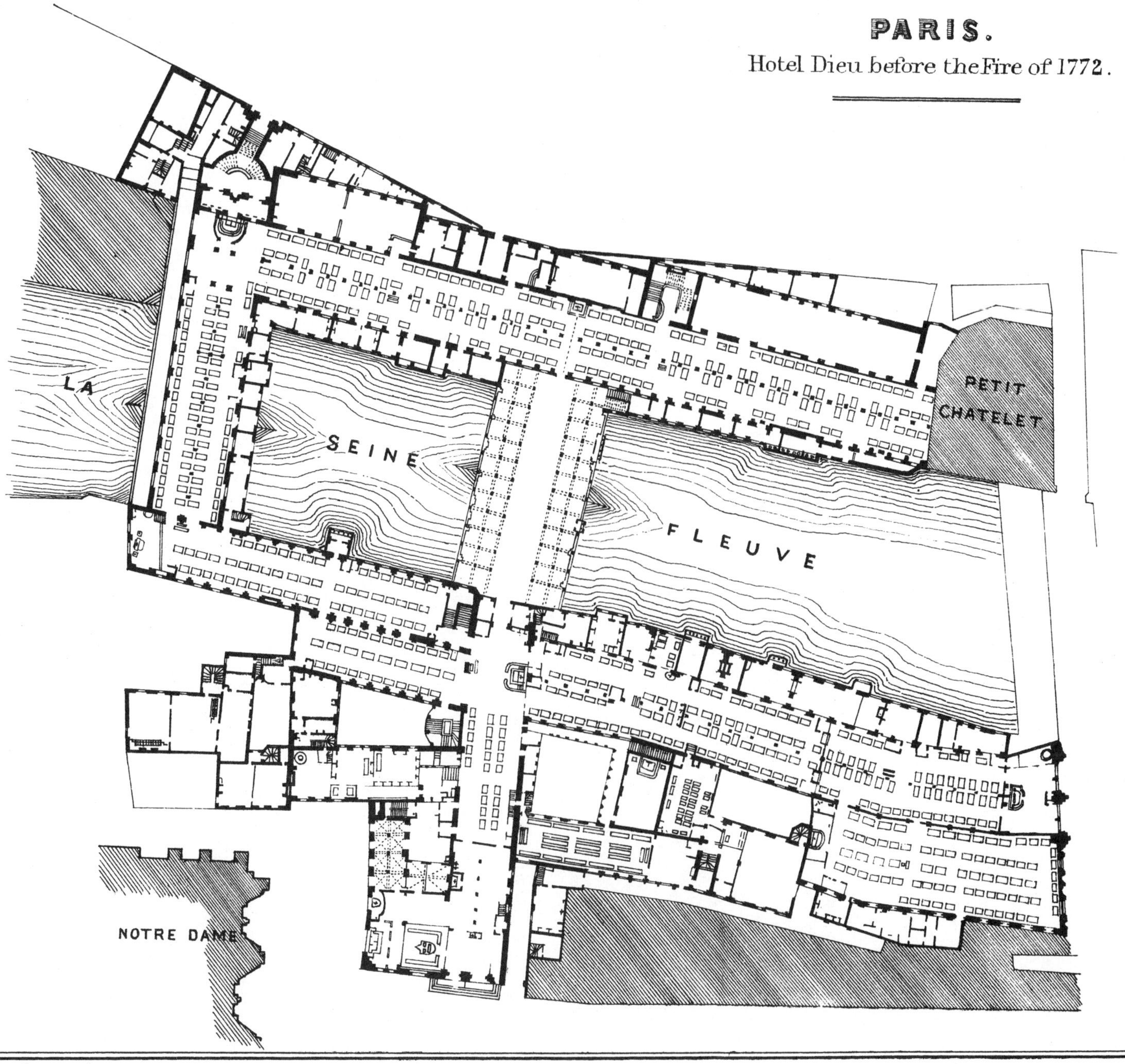

F. G. Netherclift, lith. 17 Mill Street, Conduit St. W.

London. Longman, Green & Co.

number of sick, who were sometimes placed in the beds as close together as they could lie. In this way, from 2000 to 5000 or even 7000 sick were sometimes in the hospital at one time. And one out of every four patients used to die.

So late as the year 1788, *each of the beds* in the Hôtel Dieu was intended to hold either two or four sick. There is an extremely curious notice of this subject in M. Husson's "Etude sur les Hôpitaux," given in Note C, at the end of this section. From this it appears that in the 16th century, notwithstanding the use of multiple beds, holding, in 1515, from 8 to 12 patients each, the number of sick so far exceeded the bed accommodation that the beds, in 1530, were occupied by relays of patients, and that forms were provided on which the sick whose turn it was to be out of bed could rest in the mean time.

The subject is almost too painful to dwell on, especially as we must take it for granted that the administration of the period acted according to the best of its judgment. Only let the warning be taken. And let us not reproduce, even on a small scale, the same structural defects or mismanagement which led to such terrible loss of life.

Fortunately for humanity, every patient has long since acquired the right to his own separate bed.

2. *Deficiency of Space per bed.*—Wherever cubic space is deficient, ventilation is bad. Cubic space and ventilation will therefore go hand in hand. The law holds good with regard to hospitals, barracks, and all inhabited places.

If over-crowding, or its concomitant, bad ventilation, among healthy people, generates disease, it does so to a far greater extent among the sick in hospitals. In civil hospitals the amount of cubic space varies between 600 and 2000 cubic feet per bed. In some military hospitals it used to be under 300;

and from 700 to 800 was considered a somewhat extravagant allowance. The old army practice of allotting from 600 to 800 cubic feet per bed in hospitals, under which army hospitals proved to be so unhealthy, *was* over-crowding. At Scutari, at one time, not even half the regulation-space was given; and the great over-crowding consequent thereupon was one element in the disastrous result which followed. Any one in the habit of examining hospitals with different relative amounts of cubic space cannot fail to have been struck with the very different appearance of the sick, and with the different state of the ward atmosphere. Cubic space is an essential element in the question of ventilation. It is impossible, with due regard to warmth, to ventilate a ward in a brick or stone hospital without mechanical means, when the space per bed is less than a certain amount. Crowded wards are, in fact, offensive, with all the windows open.

In airy positions in the country less cubic space is essential than in closely-built towns. In detached huts or pavilions, especially if they be but one story high, less space is necessary than where numbers are massed together in large buildings, or in more stories than one.

Under all circumstances, however, the progress of the cases (in solidly-built hospitals) will betray any curtailment of space much below 1500 cubic feet. In Paris 1700, and in London 2000 and even 2500 cubic feet are now thought advisable. But query, Should there be a hospital at all in any position which requires such an amount of space? Does not this very fact testify as loudly as it can, This is no fit place for sick?

The master of some large works in London lately mentioned the following fact:—He was in the habit of sending those of his workmen who met with accidents to two different metropolitan hospitals. In one they recovered quickly: in the other they were frequently attacked with erysipelas, and some cases were fatal. On inquiry it appeared that in the former hospital a larger amount of space was allowed than in the latter, which is also so deficient in external ventilation and in construction, that nothing but artificial ventilation could effectively change its atmosphere.

It is even more important to have a sufficient surface-area between the adjoining and the opposite beds. Piling space above the patient is not all that is wanted. In the lofty corridors of Scutari I have seen two long rows of opposite beds with scarcely three feet from foot to foot. Certainly it cannot be thought too much, under any circumstances, to give to each bed a territory to itself of at least eight feet wide by twelve or thirteen feet long.

3. *Deficiency of Ventilation.*—The want of fresh air may be detected in the appearance of patients sooner than any other want. No care or luxury will compensate indeed for its absence. Unless the air *within* the ward can be kept as fresh as it is *without*, the patients had better be away. What must then be said when, as in some town situations, the air *without* is not fresh air at all? Except in a few cases well known to physicians, the danger of admitting fresh air directly is very much exaggerated. Patients in bed are not peculiarly inclined to catch cold,* and in England, where fuel is cheap,

* 'Catching cold' in bed follows the same law as 'catching cold' when up. If the atmosphere is foul, and the lungs and skin cannot therefore relieve the system, then a draught upon the patient may give him cold. But this is the fault of the foul air, not of the fresh.

In the wooden hospital huts before Sebastopol, with their pervious walls and open ridge ventilators, in which the patients sometimes said that they 'would get less snow if they were outside,' such a thing as 'catching cold' was never heard of. The patients were well covered with blankets, and were all the better for the cold air.

somebody is indeed to blame, if the ward cannot be kept warm enough, and if the patients cannot have bed-clothing enough, for as much air to be admitted from without as suffices to keep the ward fresh. *No* artificial ventilation will do this. Although in badly-constructed hospitals, or in countries where fuel is dear, and the winter very cold, artificial ventilation may be necessary, it never can compensate for the want of the open window. The ward is never fresh, and in the best hospitals at Paris, artificially ventilated, it will be found that, till the windows are opened, the air is close. A well-waged controversy has lately been carried on upon this very point, in Paris. Eminent authorities in England had decried the pavilion system, on the ground that the atmosphere of a certain Paris pavilion hospital was "detestable," not because of the pavilion architecture, but because of its artificial ventilation defying the best pavilion building to ventilate its patients. What is all that luxury of magnificent windows for but to admit fresh air? To shut up your patients tight in artificially warmed air, is to bake them in a slow oven. Open the Lariboisière windows, warm it with open fires, drain it properly, and it will be one of the finest hospitals in the world.

Natural ventilation, or that by open windows and open fire-places, is the only efficient means for procuring the life-spring of the sick—fresh air. But to obtain this the ward should be at least fifteen to sixteen feet high, and the distance between the opposite windows not more than thirty feet. The amount of fresh air required for ventilation has been hitherto very much underrated, because it has been assumed that the quantity of carbonic acid produced during respiration was the chief noxious gas to be carried off. The total amount of this gas produced by an adult in twenty-four hours is about 40,000 cubic inches, which, in a barrack-room, say, containing sixteen men, would give 370 cubic feet *per diem*. Allowing eight hours for the night occupation of such a room, when the doors and windows may be supposed to be shut, the product of carbonic acid would be 123 cubic feet, or about fifteen and a-half cubic feet per hour. This large quantity, if not speedily carried away, would undoubtedly be injurious to health; but there are other gaseous poisons produced with the carbonic acid which have still greater power to injure. Every adult exhales by the lungs and skin forty-eight ounces, or three pints of water, in twenty-four hours. Sixteen men in a room would therefore exhale in eight hours sixteen pints of water, and 123 cubic feet of carbonic acid, into the atmosphere of the room. With the watery vapour there is also exhaled a large quantity of organic matter, ready to enter into the putrefactive condition. This is especially the case during the hours of sleep, and as it is a vital law that all excretions are injurious to health if reintroduced into the system, it is easy to understand how the breathing of damp foul air of this kind, and the consequent re-introduction of excrementitious matter into the blood through the function of respiration, will tend to produce disease.

If this be so for the well, how much more will it be so for the sick?—for the sick, the exhalations from whom are always highly morbid and dangerous, as they are one of nature's methods of eliminating noxious matter from the body, in order that it may recover health. Indeed, this is so well acknowledged that it has given rise to all the doctrine of infection—to a just horror of breathing what comes from the sick, even to the morbid fear of entering a cab in which a case of fever or small-pox has been for half an hour. Nay, we have heard a myth of scarlet fever being "carried in a bedside carpet."

One would think the inference in people's minds, from these just (and unjust) terrors, would be to remove instantly every hindrance to the foul air being carried off; but, instead of that, their inference is to shut it up or to run away from the sick.

One would think that the first and last idea in constructing hospitals would be to contrive such means of ventilation as would be perpetually and instantly carrying off these morbid emanations. One would think that it would be the first thing taught to the attendants to manage such means of ventilation. Often, however, it is *not even* the *last* thing taught to them.

A much larger mass of air is required to dilute and carry away these emanations than is generally supposed, and the whole art of ventilation resolves itself into applying in any specific case the best method of renewing the air sufficiently without producing draughts, or occasioning excessive varieties in temperature. Trifling varieties are rather beneficial than otherwise in most cases. A cooler atmosphere at night acts like a tonic.

4. *Deficiency of Light.*—What is the proportionate influence of the four defects enumerated in delaying recovery I am not competent to determine.

Second only to fresh air, however, I should be inclined to rank light in importance for the sick. Direct sunlight, not only daylight, is necessary for speedy recovery, except, perhaps, in certain ophthalmic and a small number of other cases. Instances could be given, almost endless, where, in dark wards or in wards with a northern aspect, even when thoroughlv warmed, or in wards with borrowed light, even when thoroughly ventilated, the sick could not by any means be made speedily to recover. The effect of light on health and disease has been long recognised in the medical profession as may be learned from the writings of Sir Andrew Wylie, Dr. Milne-Edwards, and Mr. Ward. Dark barrack-rooms, and barrack-rooms with northern aspects, will furnish a larger amount of sickness than light and sunny rooms.

Among kindred effects of light I may mention, from experience, as quite perceptible in promoting recovery, the being able to see out of a window, instead of looking against a dead wall; the bright colours of flowers; the being able to read in bed by the light of a window close to the bed-head. It is generally said that the effect is upon the mind. Perhaps so; but it is no less so upon the body on that account.

All hospital buildings in this climate should be erected so that as great a surface as possible should receive direct sun-light—a rule which has been observed in several of our best hospitals, but, I am sorry to say, passed over in some of those most recently constructed. Window-blinds can always moderate the light of a light ward; but the gloom of a dark ward is irremediable.

The axis of a ward should be as nearly as possible north and south; the windows on both sides, so that the sun shall shine in (from the time he rises till the time he sets) at one side or the other. There should be a window to at least every two beds, as is the case now in our best hospitals. Some foreign hospitals, in countries where the light is far more intense than in England, give one window to every bed. The window-space should be one-third of the wall-space. The windows should reach from two or three feet of the floor to one foot of the ceiling. The escape of heat may be diminished by plate or double glass. But while we *can* generate warmth, we cannot generate daylight, or the purifying and curative effect of the sun's rays.

Note A.—On the Mortality of Hospital Nurses.

To show the great importance of this point, I give the following tables, kindly prepared by Dr. Farr, from returns furnished to me with the greatest readiness by fifteen of the metropolitan hospitals. Table I. gives the ages of living and dying among the nursing staff. Table II. gives the mortality from zymotic diseases, and the comparison between the nurses' mortality and the mortality of the female population of London.

Table I.—*Numbers and Ages of Matrons, Sisters, and Nurses (Living and Dying) in Fifteen London Hospitals.*

(*Names of the hospitals,—St. Mary's; St. George's; Westminster; Charing Cross; Middlesex; University College; Royal Free; King's College; St. Bartholomew's; London; Guy's; St. Thomas'; Small Pox; Fever; and Consumption.*)

LIVING (1858).

	Total of all Ages.	Total.		Specified Ages of the Living, March, 1858.											
		Ages Specified.	Ages *not* Specified.	Under 20.	20.	25.	30.	35.	40.	45.	50.	55.	60.	65.	70 and up.
Matrons, Sisters and Nurses	521	391	130	1	10	45	55	93	64	59	34	18	8	4	...
Matrons and Sisters ...	118	90	28	...	...	4	11	22	16	20	8	5	3	1	...
Nurses	403	301	102	1	10	41	44	71	48	39	26	13	5	3	...

DYING (1848—57).

	Total of all Ages.	Total.		Ages of the Dying.											
		Ages Specified.	Ages *not* Specified.	Under 20.	20.	25.	30.	35.	40.	45.	50.	55.	60.	65.	70 and up.
Matrons, Sisters and Nurses	79	79	...	...	...	4	11	8	18	8	10	7	6	2	5
* Matrons and Sisters (so distinguished)	19	19	...	...	...	...	2	1	4	...	3	2	1	1	5
Nurses	60	60	...	...	...	4	9	7	14	8	7	5	5	1	...

* In the returns of deaths, four Hospitals do not distinguish the Matrons and Sisters from the Nurses, and in this Table they are included with the Nurses.

TABLE II.—*Table of the Mortality of Matrons, Sisters, and Nurses, at different Ages, in Fifteen London Hospitals, compared with the Mortality of the Female Population of London.*

Ages.	Matrons, Sisters, and Nurses (1848—1857).		Female Population of London.	
	Annual Rate of Mortality to 1000 living at the respective Ages.			
	By *all* returned *Diseases*.	By *Zymotic* Diseases.	By *Zymotic* Diseases (1848—57).	By *all* returned *Diseases* (1848—54).
25 to 35	15.89	9.53	2.19	9.92
35 — 45	15.80	10.94	2.73	14.65
45 — 55	17.80	11.87	3.17	20.36
55 — 65	46.36	14.26	4.94	36.02

The fatal zymotic diseases included in this table are fever and cholera, and it will be seen that these two diseases occasioned nearly 50 per cent. of the total mortality among the nursing staff as against 16 per cent. among the London female population. This single fact is quite enough to prove the very great importance of hospital hygiene. The calculated total mortality is also very much higher among the nurses, even if we assume that the deaths in the returns are all deaths due to hospital nursing, which is very doubtful. If we assume that the non-zymotic mortality among nurses ought to be the same as it is among the female population, and if to this we add the zymotic deaths among nurses, we find the total mortality among nurses to exceed the total mortality among the female population of the metropolis by about 40 per cent. The loss of a well-trained nurse by preventible disease is a greater loss than is that of a good soldier from the same cause. Money cannot replace either, but a good nurse is more difficult to find than a good soldier.

The data from which these tables have been deduced are imperfect, and it would be very desirable if in future all hospitals would keep a register of nurses. The following form would be one well calculated to give the required information. The subject is of additional importance in connexion with the proper working of a Superannuation Fund for nurses:—

Form of Register of Sisters and Nurses in Hospital. Commenced from January 1, 1859.

No.	Name.	Age when first Appointed.	Date. Of Appointment.	Date. Dismissal, Resignation, or Superannuation.	State of Health on Leaving the Service: and, if Ill, the Disease, its Duration, and probable Cause.	Date of Death, Cause of Death, and Fatal Disease.
1	Jane Jones. (Sister.)	25	June 6, 1858.	Resigned August 6, 1858.	In good Health.	
2	Mary Evans. (Nurse.)	29	April 2, 1848.			July 7, 1854, Typhoid Fever, after 11 days' illness.

NOTE B.—ON THE HISTORY OF THE DOCTRINE OF CONTAGION.

The history of the doctrine of 'Contagion' is given by Dr. Adams in his translation of the works of Paulus Ægineta, vol. 1, p. 284—(Sydenham Society). He says, in his comment, "the earlier ancient authors appear to have entertained no suspicions of contagion as a cause of febrile or of other complaints.

"The works of the fathers of history and of medicine have likewise been ransacked in vain for any traces of the doctrine of contagion."

Thucydides, and after him several of the Latin poets, describe the plague of Athens, which appears to have been a form of Dysentery, as communicable from person to person. The later Greek historians contain allusions to the infectious nature of certain diseases; but Procopius, though cognizant of one of the greatest pestilences on record, was a non-contagionist.

Virgil's allusions to contagious diseases among cattle will be found in Ecl. I. Georg. III., 464.

Aretæus appears to be the first medical author who believed in contagion. Galen seems to have held the doctrine of infection. Of the later Greek and Arabian medical writers, some were contagionists, and others make no allusion to the subject. Dr. Adams states, in regard to plague, a disease which, in later times, has been considered as the very type of all "contagious" pestilences, "The result of our investigations into the opinions of the ancients on this subject leads us to the conclusion that all, or at least the most intelligent of the medical authorities, held that the plague was communicated not by any specific virus, but in consequence of the atmosphere around the sick being contaminated by putrid effluvia."

The obvious practical result of this view of infection is that abundance of pure air will prevent infection. All my own hospital experience confirms this conclusion. If infection exists, it is preventible. If it exists, it is the result of carelessness, or of ignorance. "Contagion," as a doctrine, on which distinct practical proceedings have been taken, appears to be of very modern invention; and it has been highly injurious to civilization and humanity, from the loss of life which has from time to time followed from the practices which it inculcates, and from the immense tax which it has entailed upon commerce.

NOTE C.

"IN 1788" (in the Hôtel Dieu), "each bed was for two or for four sick."

"Much has been said about beds in two shelves, one over the other, in which up to eight and even twelve sick were said to have lain. Nothing in the Archives justifies such an assertion. This tradition, derived from M. de Pastoret, doubtless originated in a passage of the Report of the Commissioners of the Académie des Sciences (1786, p. 19), where it is said that in 1752 the sick were four and six in the same bed, and that some were lying on the testers of the beds, 'according to the testimony of a physician of the Hôtel Dieu, who witnessed it.' This testimony is the more curious, because the 'Mémoire of the Physicians of the Hôtel Dieu,' presented in 1756, makes no allusion to this circumstance, although the form of the beds takes up a very large share of the Report.

"That, at times of extraordinary over-crowding, some of the sick should have been placed even on the wooden roof of the bed, as in 1752, when the Hôtel Dieu had to receive more than 4000 sick, this fact would not be very surprising; but this was only a momentary expedient, and can only have taken place, if it did take place, from the period of the 17th century; for before that period the beds of the Hôtel Dieu had no testers. It was then in beds that the sick lay, or rather were heaped up. In 1515, there were only 303 beds at the Hôtel Dieu, 'in each of which, from want of space, are generally seen eight, ten, and twelve poor in one bed, so crowded that it is a great pity to see them.' "—(Letters Patent of Francis I., 1515.)—(*Archives of the Assistance Publique.*)

" 100 beds were placed in the new ward built by Cardinal Duprat in 1530. The following is an extract of the bargain made for the construction of these beds.

"Jehan Morel, carpenter, living at Paris, has bargained with the Governors to make proper beds to furnish the new ward which the Legate is building to adjoin Lostel-Dieu, *i.e.*, up to the number of 100 beds, made as follows :—Each bed 6 feet long by 4 feet wide, the back 4 feet high, the division (or partition) the same height, all in plain panel, and all framed and open below; in the front of which beds two horizontal panels, ... on the pillow of which beds there shall be a board 6 inches in breadth or thereabouts, for the service of the poor; under each of which beds there shall be a little form (bench) of the length of said beds, to be taken out to rest the said poor."

(Extract from the Registers, 1533.) The sick, being too many to lie all together in the same bed, necessarily relieved each other. And this little bench was no doubt intended to serve as a seat for those who were waiting their turn to lie down.

" In the 17th century, the beds of the Hôtel Dieu were covered with a tester standing upon four massive feet, with curtains which, when drawn, completely shut in the bed.

"In 1781, Louis XVI. forbade more than two sick being placed in the same bed, and these were to be separated by a compartment or division. This did not satisfy the physicians of the Hôtel Dieu, and it was decided,

"1. That all the beds, single and double, should be 6½ feet high.

2. That all beds, single and double, should be 6 feet long over all.

'3. That all single beds should be uniformly 3 feet wide over all.

"4. That all double beds should be alike 5 feet 2 inches wide over all.

"5. That the testers of all the said beds should have a strong cross-beam, for a cord to be solidly fastened, by which the sick can raise themselves."—(*Deliberations, etc.*, 1781.)

"In 1791, the number of beds was still far from enough, as states a Report of the Commission of Hospitals:—'In April, 1791, there were only 1650 to 1700 beds, of which 580 to 590 were large beds; counting these for two, as well as those with divisions, the 1700 beds gave about room for 2300 sick; the sick who had a bed a-piece being only 1700; 1100 others lay 2, 3, and even more in the large beds.'" (Report of the measures taken to accommodate at the Hôtel Dieu, during the winter of 1792, 2500 sick, of whom 2000 in little beds, one in each bed, and 500 in large beds, *only two* together.—*Archives of the Assistance Publique.*)

II.

DEFECTS IN EXISTING HOSPITAL PLANS AND CONSTRUCTION.

CONSIDERING, then, that the conditions essential to the health of hospitals are principally these—

1. Fresh Air. 2. Light. 3. Ample Space. 4. Subdivision of Sick into Separate Buildings or Pavilions—let us examine the causes in the usual ward construction which prevent us from obtaining these and other necessary conditions. The principal causes are as follow, viz.:—

1. Selection of Bad Sites and Bad Local Climates for Hospitals.

2. Construction of Hospitals on such a plan as to prevent Free Circulation of External Air.

3. Defects in Ward Construction injurious to Ventilation including:—Defective Height of Wards; excessive Width of Wards between the Opposite Windows; arranging the Beds along the Dead Walls; having more than two Rows of Beds between the opposite Windows; having Windows only on one Side, or having a closed Corridor connecting the Wards.

4. Defective Means of Natural Ventilation and Warming.

5. Defects of Drainage, Waterclosets, Sinks, &c.

6. Using Absorbent Materials for Walls and Ceilings, and Washing Floors of Hospitals.

7. Defective Hospital Kitchens.

8. Defective Hospital Laundries.
9. Defective Accommodation for Nursing and Discipline.
10. Defective Ward Furniture.

1. *Selection of Bad Sites and Bad Local Climates for Hospitals.*—As the object to be attained in hospital construction is to have pure dry air for the sick, it will be evident that this condition cannot be fulfilled if a damp climate be selected. It is a well-known fact, *e.g.*, that in the more damp localities of the south of England, certain classes of sick and of invalids linger, and do not recover their health. Again, retentive clay subsoils keep the air over entire districts of the country always more or less damp. And soils of this character should not be selected as sites for hospitals. Self-draining, gravelly, or sandy subsoils are best. River banks, estuary shores, valleys, marshy or muddy ground, ought to be avoided. It may seem superfluous to state that a hospital should not be built over an old graveyard, or on other ground charged with organic matter, and yet this has been recently done. Although hospitals are intended for the recovery of health, people are very apt to forget this, and to be guided in the selection of sites by other considerations—such as cheapness, convenience, and the like; whereas, the professed object in view being to secure the recovery of the sick in the shortest time, and to obtain the smallest mortality, that object should be distinctly kept in view as one which must take precedence of all others.

Similar remarks are applicable to the erection of hospitals in large cities and towns. If the recovery of the sick *simply* is to be the object of hospitals, they will not be built among dense unhealthy populations. If medical schools are the object, surely it is more instructive for students to watch the recovery from, rather than the lingering in, sickness. Twice the number of cases would be brought under their notice in a hospital in which the sick recovered in half the time necessary in another.

According to all analogy, the duration of cases, the chances against complete recovery, and, as has been shown, the rate of mortality, must be greater in town than in country hospitals.

Land in towns is too expensive for hospitals to be so built as to secure the conditions of ventilation and of light, and of spreading the inmates over a large surface-area—conditions now known to be essential to speedy recovery—instead of piling them up three or four stories high, in regions contaminated with coal smoke and nuisances.

In country towns, and even in the larger manufacturing and commercial towns, there is no great difficulty in building hospitals in the purer atmosphere of the open country or suburbs. The distance from any part of the town likely to send its sick or maimed can never be very great; and gratuitous medical and surgical service can be rendered without much inconvenience by the officers of the hospital. The distance, also, to be traversed by friends on visiting days is not so great as to cause undue loss of time. No legitimate excuse can therefore be urged for constructing hospitals amid the smoke, foul air, and bustle of the densely-peopled seats of commerce and manufactures. It is otherwise with such a place as London. Here the distances are so great, and the outward spread of the population so rapid, that the question of hospital position assumes quite another aspect to what it does in provincial towns. The problem has been, besides, complicated by the nature of the hospital Foundations, which have been created at different periods of time, and under very different conditions of population. The various metropolitan hospitals have been erected, and their positions determined on no general system of medical or surgical relief for the metropolis, and without any foresight, had it even been possible to exercise such, as to what would finally be the position of each hospital with reference to the population whose sick it was intended to receive.

The practical result has been, that several of the largest and most important hospital establishments are concentrated within a comparatively narrow area of the metropolitan district. They receive their sick from a certain radius in every direction, extending often into and even beyond the district which would be allotted to other hospitals under a general system of hospital relief. And they receive their patients from distances of two, three, five, or more miles, or even from the country round.

To illustrate this question as regards our metropolitan hospitals, I give a sketch-plan of London, on which are shown the distances of all the larger hospitals in direct lines from one central point, St. Paul's. Four hospitals only out of twenty-one are nearer than a mile. All the others are at distances varying from a mile to nearly five miles. The map shows that there are large areas of the metropolis which have to send their sick even greater distances than the average required by the French system, presently to be noticed; and that, practically, the question of distance has been little understood in controversies which have arisen on this subject.

One result which follows from this arrangement of the London hospitals is, that a considerable proportion of the sick has been concentrated towards the heart of the metropolis, not unfrequently among dense masses of population and in unhealthy localities. It may be safely stated that, if all the existing general hospitals had been originally distributed at suitable distances from the middle of the metropolis, they would all have been placed as conveniently for the sick as they now are, and in much purer air. The question of moving existing hospitals has been mooted at different times, and has recently assumed a practical shape as regards one of them, St. Thomas's. A long and warm controversy has arisen on the subject, in which nearly every element incident to such questions has been discussed, with the ultimate probability that the future site of the hospital will be determined by no element incident to the question, but by circumstances only. It is worth while to consider briefly the main points which have been mooted in this important controversy.

The elements which ought to determine the position of a hospital are the following:—

First, and before all others, purity of the atmosphere.

Second, the possibility of conveying the sick and maimed to it.

Third, accessibility for medical officers, and for the friends of the sick.

Fourth, convenient position for a medical school, if there be one.

All of these elements are of importance, every one in its place. It is obviously of no use to build a hospital in the best air in the world, if neither patients nor medical officers can get to it. It is only in applying common sense to such a question, and by always giving a preponderance to the condition of highest importance—namely, pure air, when the other conditions can be at the same time reasonably obtained, that the best will be done for the sick.

There is no doubt that suburban sites, nearest to the population likely to apply for relief, afford the best solution the case admits of with the ordinary means of conveyance. This is to a certain extent the system in Paris. Several of its best hospitals are in or close to the suburbs, and the sick are admitted under a rule which requires all applicants to appear before the medical officers at a central bureau, whence they are sent to the hospitals where there are vacant beds. Accidents and other cases of urgency may, however, be admitted at once into any hospital on certificate of one of the hospital physicians or surgeons. It will be seen that under this system the patient has to leave his home and present himself at the bureau, and from the bureau he has to go to the hospital. Some of the establishments are at a considerable distance from the bureau.

To illustrate the working of this system, I give a sketch-plan of Paris, showing the position of the Bureau of Admission, close to the Hôtel Dieu, the distance in yards (in a direct line) from this Bureau to each of the civil hospitals, and the number of beds they contain. It will be seen that four hospitals only are within a mile of the Bureau, and that the remaining twelve are at distances of from a mile and a half to two miles and a half in straight lines, to which probably a fourth should be added for bendings of streets, and from a third to a half for the average distance between the houses of the patients and the Bureau. There appears to be no practical difficulty attending this, so far at least as the distance is concerned; but, as already stated, urgent cases are admitted at any hospital at once on the certificate of a medical officer.

Of course the distances are all much less in Paris than they would be in London with a similar organization, and yet there are several special hospitals in London—*e.g.*, those for consumption, small-pox, and fever—which are at a far greater distance from some of the districts yielding them cases, than are the distances in Paris.

All are agreed that fresh country air is better for the sick than impure town air, and hence the whole question narrows itself within the compass of one of the conditions enumerated above—namely, accessibility. Any site which can be obtained, with pure air and sufficiently convenient means of access, will fulfil the required conditions. It has been proposed to extend the distance by using railway conveyance. To this there can be no possible objection, if it is necessary. A few years ago no one could have predicated that a considerable portion of the metropolitan dead would be conveyed long distances by railway for interment, without inconvenience to friends, or injury to their feelings, and yet it has been done. The truth is, however, that in regard to hospital sites, no precise general rule can be laid down.

If a new hospital is wanted, the true way to deal with the question is to determine whereabouts it must be; next, to seek out all the sites which there is a possibility of obtaining; then to have each examined by competent persons with reference to the elements already laid down, and to select the best.

This has been done in selecting recent hospital sites, and it has answered well enough in practice. The evil arising out of a contrary procedure is, that parties are apt to be formed, especially among persons who are not sufficiently acquainted with the subject: one party advocating one site, another party another, and so the cause which all have at heart is injured.

If we could suppose such a thing as all the metropolitan hospitals being removed to the furthest accessible healthy points from their present positions, there cannot be a doubt that the sick would gain immensely by the change, except accidents or cases of severe and sudden illness. For these cases special wards would have to be provided at the points where they would be most required. There is no reason why all such cases should not be treated in this way, and sent to the suburban hospitals as soon as they were able to bear the journey. The hospital receiving-rooms and dispensaries for out-patients might be attached to these accident wards.

Patients from the country would, of all others, benefit most by such a change, for they would be spared the additional risk of coming from the fresh air of their homes into the foul air of the metropolis—a change attended with more or less additional risk to them.

Even medical education would benefit by such a change. The quiet and studious habits of a college would be substituted for the desultory lecture-hunting and hospital-walking of London. Education might thus take the place of simple instruction.

2. *Construction of Hospitals on such a Plan as to prevent Free Circulation of External Air.*—To build a hospital with one closed court with high walls, or what is worse, with two closed courts, is to stagnate the air even before it reaches the wards.

This defect is one of the most serious that can be committed in hospital architecture; and it exists, nevertheless, in some form or other in nearly all the older hospitals, and in many even of recent construction.

The air outside the hospital cannot be maintained in a state sufficiently pure to be used for internal ventilation, unless there be entire freedom of movement. Anything which interferes with this is injurious. Neighbouring high walls, smoking chimneys, trees, high ground, are all more or less hurtful; but worse than all is bad construction of the hospital itself.

Examples of bad plan and construction are common enough. One of these (Fig. 1) is a block plan of the Hôpital Necker at Paris.

FIG. 1.

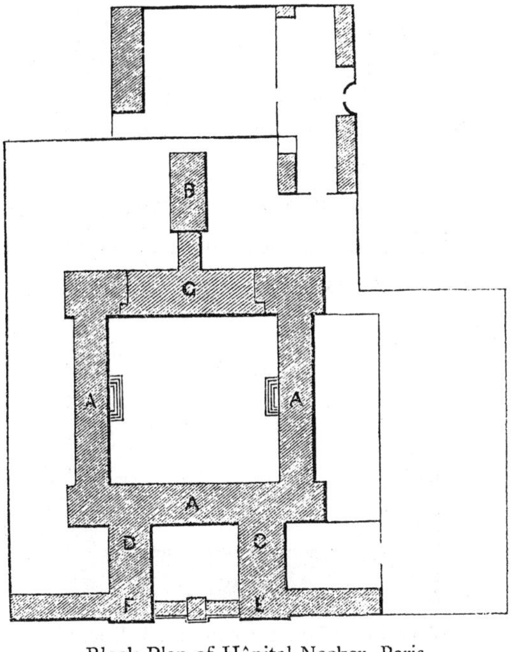

Block Plan of Hôpital Necker, Paris.

A. Wards.
B. Chapel.
C. Kitchen.
D. Pharmacy.
E. Offices and "Sisters."
F. Dwellings.
G. Gallery.

In this case, it is true, the size of the inner court is so considerable that, to a certain extent, it obviates the objection. But where this principle of construction is applied in smaller buildings, the evil of it becomes obvious. Fig. 2 represents another form of the same defective plan. None of these arrangements should ever be used for hospitals.

FIG. 2.

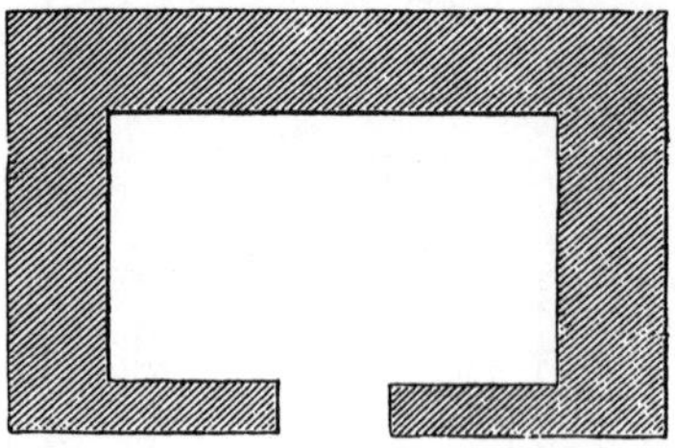

Block Plan of the Royal Free Hospital, London.

All closed corners stagnate the air, more or less, even where the building forms but three sides of a square, as in Fig. 3, unless the wings are so short that they can hardly be called wings.

FIG. 3.

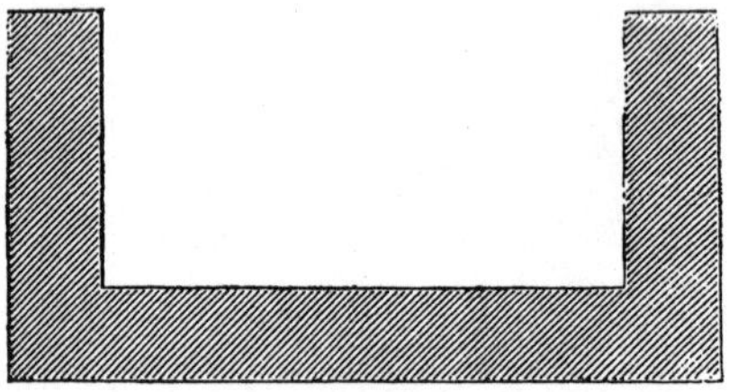

Block Plan of the London Hospital, London.

The only safe plan, with this form of construction, is to leave the corners entirely open, as in Vincennes plan, where they are connected only by an arcade on the ground floor. (Plan No. 5.)

Even in the true separate pavilion structure, unless the distance between the pavilions be double the height of the walls, the ventilation and light are seriously interfered with.

For this, among other reasons, two stories are better than three; and one is preferable to two, provided it be erected upon an arched basement.

To build a hospital in the midst of a crowded neighbourhood of narrow streets and high houses, is to ensure a stagnation of the air without, which no ventilation within, no cubic space, however ample, will be able to remedy.

I shall return to this subject in discussing the question of what should be the relative position of different parts of a hospital.

3. *Defects in Ward Construction injurious to Ventilation.*—One of the most common causes of unhealthiness in hospitals is defective construction and arrangement of the ward-space of such a nature as to lead to difficulty of ventilation, or want of light. The expression, "a good ward," comprehends something quite different from mere appearance. No ward is in any sense a good ward in which the sick are not at all times supplied with pure air, light, and a due temperature. These are the results to be obtained from hospital architecture, and not external design or appearance. Again, no one of these elements need be sacrificed in seeking to obtain another. Any one who feels himself in a difficulty in realizing all three may rest satisfied that hospital architecture is not his vocation. A few of the more common errors may be here introduced as illustrative of this part of the subject:—

Defective Height of Wards.—It is not possible to ventilate sufficiently a large ward of ten or twelve feet high. And again, it is not possible to ventilate a ward where there is a great height above the windows. A ward of thirty beds can be well ventilated with a height of about fifteen or sixteen feet, provided the windows reach to within one foot of the ceiling. Otherwise, the top of the ward becomes a reservoir for foul air. But a ward may be too high to be ventilated with sufficient ease. Good ventilation consists in emptying the hospital of foul air as speedily as possible. Why have a greater height of ward than will allow the windows and ventilating arrangements to be easily managed? It is more than probable that the decrease of facility for opening windows would lead to negligence, and so to the fine lofty ward becoming a reservoir of foul air.

Too Great Width of Wards between the Opposite Windows.—It does not appear as if the air could be thoroughly changed, if a distance of more than thirty feet intervenes between the opposite windows: if, in other words, the ward is more than thirty feet wide. This is the true starting-point from which to determine the size of your ward, and the number of beds you will have in it. If you make your length too great in proportion to this width, your ward becomes a tunnel—a form fatal to good ventilation. This was the case with the great corridor wards at Scutari.

If, on the other hand, you make your wards too short in proportion to this width, you multiply corners in a greater ratio than you multiply sick. And direct experiment has shown that the movement of the air in the centre of a ward is three or four times as great as it is at the corners. The movement of the air in a hospital ward should always be slightly perceptible over the face and hands, and yet there should be no draughts.

Arranging the Beds along the Dead Walls.—This deprives the patient of the amount of light and air necessary to his recovery, and has, besides, the disadvantage that when the windows are opened the effluvia must blow over all the intervening beds before escaping. This arrangement is to be seen at Portsmouth Military Hospital (Fig. 4), Chatham Garrison

Plan No. II.

GROUND PLAN OF THE SOUTH EASTERN WING OF THE ROYAL VICTORIA HOSPITAL, NETLEY,

SHOWING ONE SIDE OF EACH WARD COVERED BY AN EXTERNAL CORRIDOR.

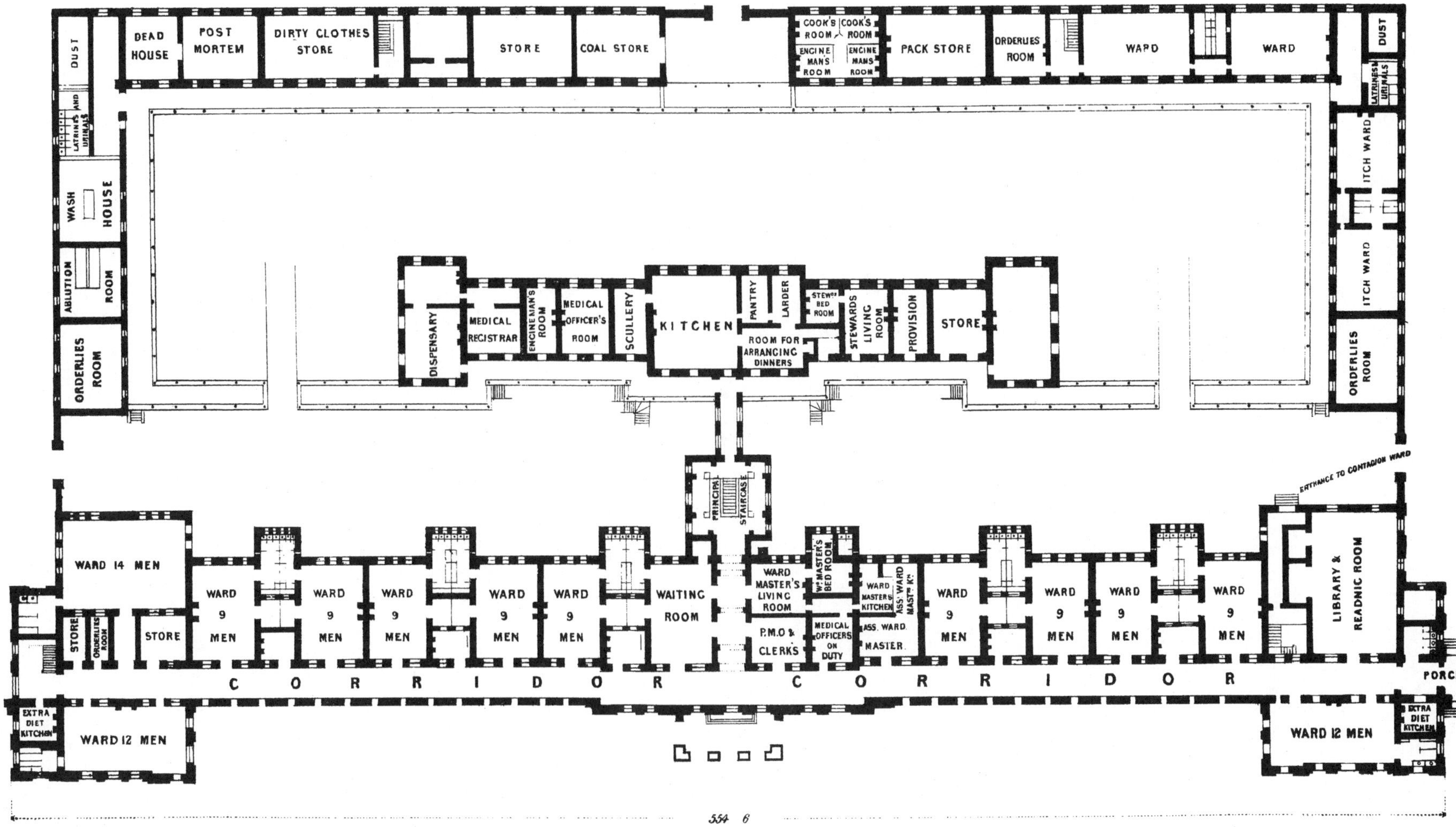

Scale 60 Feet to One Inch

0 10 20 40 60 80 100 200 Feet

London. Longman, Green & Co.

Hospital, in the new part of the Edinburgh Infirmary, and at Netley Hospital. (Plan 2.)

FIG. 4.

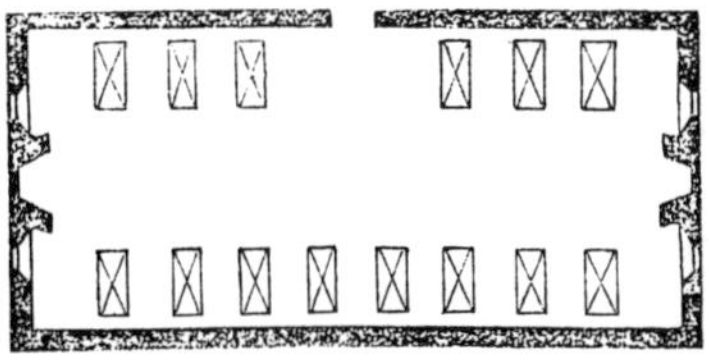

Ward Construction—Portsmouth Military Hospital.

Another striking example of the same defect is given in Fig. 5, which formerly existed in the Accouchement Hospital at Paris.

FIG. 5.

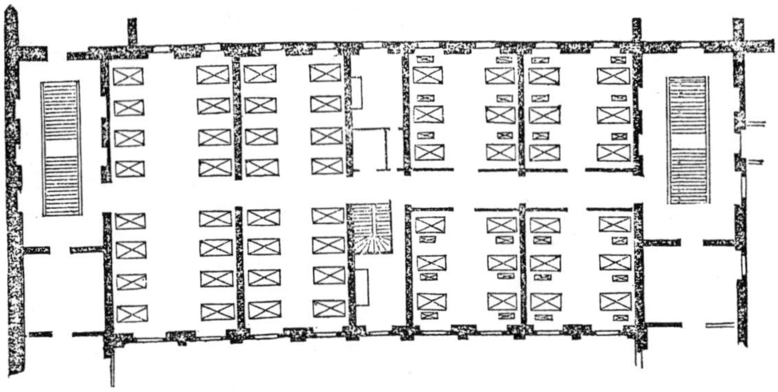

Hôpital de la Clinique, Paris.
(Former arrangement of Lying-in Wards.)

Unfortunately, we have not to go abroad for existing examples of this construction. The following plan (fig. 6), which represents the arrangement of a floor of Manchester Royal Infirmary, will tell its own tale.

It will be seen that in all these examples free renewal of the air is impossible, except for the beds close to the windows. It is needless to point out that plans of this kind should be

FIG. 6.

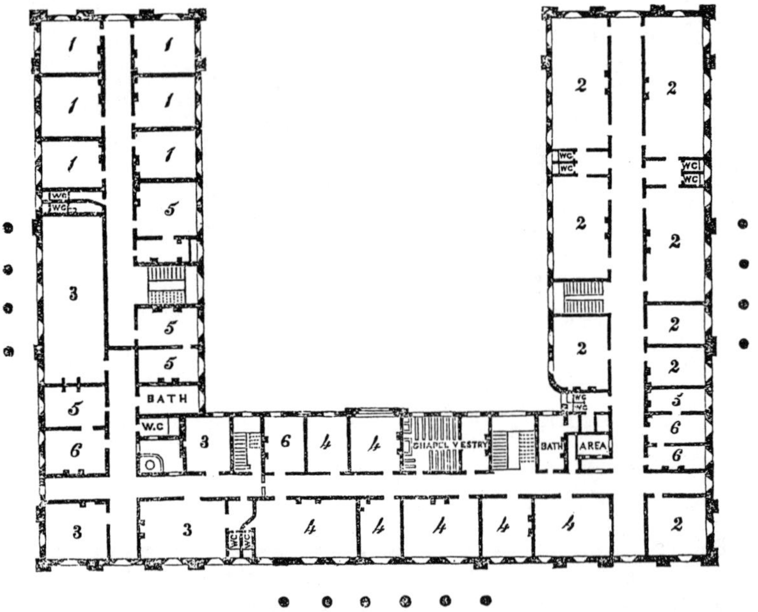

Manchester Royal Infirmary.

1. Fever wards (female.)
2. Surgical do. do.
3. Medical do. (male.)
4. Medical wards (female.)
5. Nurses' rooms.
6. Do. kitchens.

abandoned in future. Another form of this arrangement is shown in Fig. 7, part of the old Marine Hospital at Woolwich. In this example there is no provision for

FIG. 7.

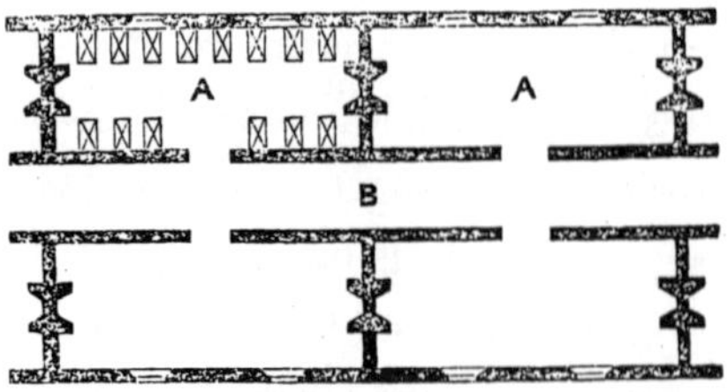

Wards of old Marine Hospital, Woolwich.

A A. Wards. B. Interior passage.

ventilation worthy of the name, and the wards are so arranged that the sick must of necessity be supplied with common foul air.

Having more than Two Rows of Beds between the Windows.—In the double wards, or wards back to back, of the new part of Guy's, of King's College, and of the Fever Hospital, this arrangement is seen. It is objectionable on every account. These double wards are from twelve to nearly twenty feet wider than they ought to be between the opposite windows for thorough ventilation. The partition down the middle with apertures makes matters rather worse; complaint has been made that it beats down the draught on the heads of the inner rows of patients. It also prevents the head nurse from having that view of her whole ward at once, which she ought to have for proper care of it. The following illustration, Fig. 8, from King's College Hospital, will show how these defects are produced.

FIG. 8.

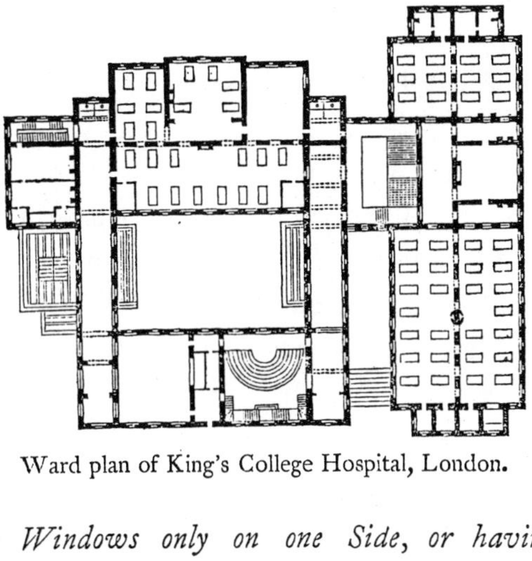

Ward plan of King's College Hospital, London.

Having Windows only on one Side, or having a closed Corridor connecting the Wards.—As it is a necessity of hospital construction that every ward must have direct communication with the external air by means of a sufficient number of windows on its opposite sides, and that every ward must have its own ventilation distinct and separate from that of every other ward; it follows that to have a dead wall on one side, or to cover one of the sides by a corridor, is directly to interfere with the natural ventilation of the ward. To join all the ward doors and windows on one side by means of a corridor is much more objectionable than even to have a dead wall, because the foul air of all the wards must necessarily pass into the corridor, and from the corridor into the wards indiscriminately. The whole hospital becomes in this way a complicated ward; and hence, without extraordinary precautions, such as are not usually nor likely to be bestowed on such matters, these corridors are the certain means of engendering a hospital atmosphere. A similar objection exists against any form of hospital construction in which a door connects any two wards. If any one had wished to see the corridor plan in all its horrors, Scutari would have shown them to him on a colossal scale. But the evils connected with corridors may be seen on a smaller scale in some part of almost every hospital in London. Netley also has its corridor. (*Vide* Plan No. 2.)

I give another illustration, Fig. 9, from the Hôpital St. Antoine, at Paris, in which it will be seen that the corridor, as well as the wards, is occupied by sick.

This building was not, however, constructed for a hospital. The arrangement is obviously a bad one.

Here is too another quite recent illustration, Fig. 10, of a grave structural defect in the new part of Glasgow Infirmary. The intention in this instance was evidently to

FIG. 9.

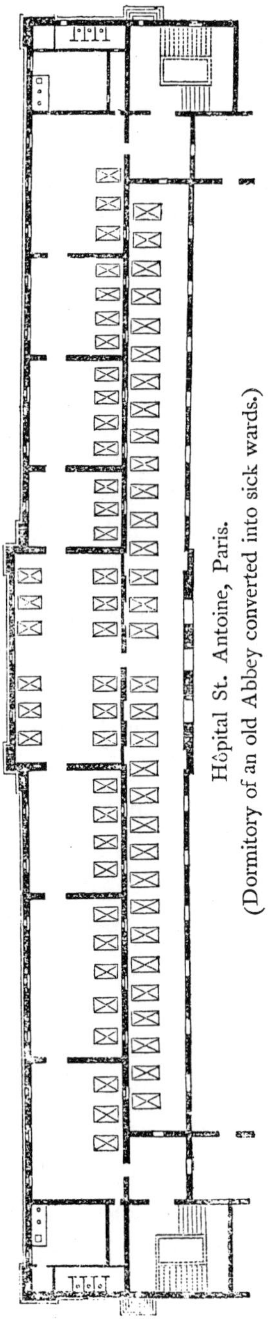

Hôpital St. Antoine, Paris.
(Dormitory of an old Abbey converted into sick wards.)

FIG. 10.

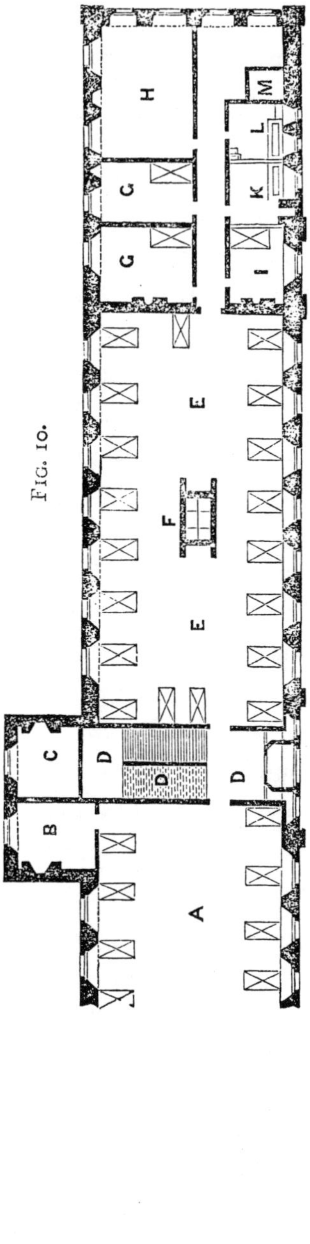

New part of Glasgow Royal Infirmary.
(Small wards, &c., entering from large wards.)

A. E. Wards.
B. I. Nurses' rooms.
C. Pupil.
D. Stair.
F. Chimney and ventilating shaft.
G. Small wards.
H. Day-room.
K, L. Baths, lavatories, water-closet.
M. Lift.

adopt sound principles of construction, but it will be observed that at one end of the ward there are three beds, and at the other four beds between the opposite windows. The small wards, intended for the most serious cases, are placed in the vicinity of the sinks, baths, and water-closet, and have a direct communication with the ventilation of the larger wards. These arrangements are to be regretted, on account of the example.

All of these defects in plan and construction of wards have a very serious influence on the question of defective ventilation and warming, which we will now discuss.

4. *Defective Means of Ventilation and Warming.*—When the question of ventilation first assumed a practical shape in this country, it was supposed that 600 cubic feet of air per hour were sufficient for a healthy adult, in a room where a number of people are congregated together. Subsequent experience, however, has shown that this is by no means enough. As much as 1000 cubic feet have been found insufficient to keep the air free from closeness and smell; and it is highly probable that the actual quantity required will ultimately be found to be at least 1500 cubic feet per hour per man.

In sick wards we have more positive experience as to the quantity of air required to keep them sweet and healthy. It was found in a certain Parisian hospital, in which the ventilating arrangements were deficient, that pyæmia and hospital gangrene had appeared among the patients. These diseases are said to have disappeared, on the introduction of ventilating arrangements, whereby 2500 cubic feet of air per bed per hour were supplied to the wards. Notwithstanding this large quantity, however, the ward-atmosphere was found not to be sufficiently pure. In other wards the quantity of air was increased to as much as 4000 or 5000 cubic feet per bed per hour. But again we say, do not trust to artificial means; without natural ventilation the air will never be *fresh*.

I have, in a preceding page, stated generally the importance, of the method of ventilation and warming employed, to the state of the ward-atmosphere. I will only repeat here, that if our object be to obtain a wholesome state of the air round the sick, we must have no air except what comes direct by windows or ventilating openings from the outer atmosphere, and we must have no other warming apparatus than the open fireplace. It is the safest warmer and ventilator. Air cooked by metal surfaces is especially to be avoided. It seems likely that we shall soon be enabled to have open fireplaces in the middle of wards, the draught being carried under the floor. It is obvious that fireplaces in the side walls are in the wrong place. There is great loss and unequal distribution of heat in consequence. But in order to obtain the benefit of a central fireplace, it is certainly not necessary to carry the chimney stalks up in the wards as has been done at Glasgow and in one Guards' hospital in London, making it look more like an Egyptian temple than a hospital.

5. *Defects in Drainage, Water Closets, Sinks, &c.*—Hospital Sewers may become cesspools of the most dangerous description, if improperly made and placed. In one hospital I knew, if the wind changed so as to blow up the open mouths of the sewers, such change was frequently marked by outbreaks of fever among the patients, and by relapses among the convalescents from fever. Where there are no means for externally ventilating the sewers, no traps, no sufficient water supply, no means for cleansing or flushing them, and where the bottoms are rough and uneven, such occurrences cannot fail to take place. The emanations from the deposits in the sewers are in such cases blown back through the pipe-drains into the water-

closets and sinks, and thence into the wards. Where sewers pass close to or under occupied rooms, the walls or covers being defective, exhalations will infallibly escape into those rooms. There are hospitals where such things exist at the present time.

There can be no safety for the sick if any but water-closets of the best construction are used, as also if they are not built *externally* to the main building, and cut off by a lobby, separately lighted and ventilated by cross windows, from the ward. The same thing may be said of sinks. I have known outbreaks of fever even among the healthy from an ill-constructed and ill-placed sink in this country.

The smell of latrines, which are not waterclosets, as used in French hospitals, is quite perceptible at the end of the ward nearest to them, and becomes, indeed, a very serious taint to the atmosphere, which might, with proper water-closets, be secured so fresh by their admirable plan of building in pavilions.

The whole drainage should be carefully studied and provided for, otherwise one may build a magnificent hospital, with abundant ventilation, and yet be distilling foul air from sewers into every ward of it.

Not very long ago five fatal cases of fever occurred in rapid succession among the nurses in one of our civil hospitals, which were traced to a defective drain.

6. *Using Absorbent Materials for Floors, Walls, and Ceilings of Hospitals, and Washing Floors.*—The amount of organic matter given off by respiration and in other ways from the sick is such that the floors, walls, and ceilings of hospital wards — if not of impervious materials — become dangerous absorbents.

The boards are in time saturated with organic matter,

from this cause, as well as from accidental filth, and want of due attention to cleansing, and only require moisture to give off noxious effluvia. When the floors are being washed, the smell of something quite other than soap and water is perfectly perceptible, and there cannot be a doubt that washing dirty floors is one cause of erysipelas, &c., in some hospitals.

Common plaster is the material most usually employed for ward walls and ceilings. The objection to it is its being porous, and its faculty of absorbing emanations from the sick. When the surface is recently finished, plaster thus tends to purify the air of a sick ward. But, after a time, it becomes saturated with impurity. Occasionally a minute vegetation appears upon it, which can be scraped off and examined by the microscope, and also chemically. When ward walls and ceilings become fouled in this way, hospital diseases are very apt to invade the wards. It has happened that workmen employed in scraping and cleansing such wards have themselves suffered from severe illness. The usual remedy is frequent lime-washing with periodical scraping. Caustic lime decomposes the organic matter or covers it with a thin film for the time. The process is objectionable, because to be of use it requires to be frequently repeated, and the wards to be evacuated during the cleansing and drying. The latter part of the process requires to be very complete, before the ward is re-occupied, to prevent accidents to the sick.

Plastered walls when not cleansed sufficiently, have led to increased impurity of the ward-air, and to hospital diseases.

7. *Defective Hospital Kitchens.*—Two facts every careful observer can establish from experience.

1. The necessity for variety in food, as an essential ele-

ment of health, owing to the number of materials required to restore and preserve the human frame. In sickness it is still more important, because, the frame being in a morbid state, it is scarcely possible to prescribe beforehand with certainty what it will be able to digest and assimilate. The so-called 'fancies' of disease are in many cases valuable indications.

2. The importance of cooking so as to secure the greatest digestibility and the greatest economy in nutritive value of food.

Feeling the importance of this element in recovery, I have often been surprised by the primitive kitchens of some of our civil hospitals, with which little variety of cooking is possible. It shows how little diet and cooking are yet thought of as sanitary and curative agents. There still exists a confusion of ideas about 'spoiling' the sick, about 'too much indulgence' of the patients, and even yet comparatively little is practically known as to what is, and what is not, essential for restoration to health.

A hospital cook, instead of being the best obtainable cook, is sometimes put to the work because she is fit for little or nothing else, and her utensils are often as faulty as her performances. I have often seen the sick unable to eat the messes prepared for them in the name of diets, not so much because they were bad in quality, as because the cook had no clear idea of the class of stomachs for which he or she had to provide. It is singular that, while so much care is taken to provide good medicine properly made up, so little care is bestowed on the cooking of that which is of more importance than most medicines. The nurse or doctor only finds out, perhaps next day, that the patient has lost appetite, or been sick, or has had a relapse, and nobody suspects that the men or women in the kitchen had occasioned it.

Steps have been taken to educate hospital cooks for the army, so that in this department of the public service there will be less chance of the sick suffering, as I have seen them suffer, than there was formerly.

But the generality of civil hospital kitchens have little to boast of; and defective hospital kitchens and bad cooking may be classed as among the causes of hospital unhealthiness. Besides this, the kitchen is not unfrequently situated in objectionable proximity to the wards: at the foot of a staircase leading to them, if not under them. This should not be. In all, except the smallest class of hospitals for a few beds only, the kitchen should be detached, to keep the damp and fumes of cooking away from the sick.

8. *Defective Hospital Laundries.*—Not very long ago there was scarcely an army hospital which had such a thing as a laundry. The bedding was washed by contract. And the body linen in the smaller hospitals was generally washed, if such a term ought to be used, in a small wash-house, or lean-to shed, with or without a boiler, and without any means for drying, getting-up, or airing linen. The linen was taken out of the damp wash-house, possibly into the damp air, and there hung up for a longer or a shorter time; and if the 'orderly' were careful of his patients, he would complete the process by drying the linen, before it was put on, in front of the ward fire. In provincial hospitals, even of our largest cities, there is sometimes a too infrequent change of bed linen; and fresh patients have been put into the last patients' sheets.

The Barrack and Hospital Improvement Commission has led to great changes, still in progress, in this important part of hospital administration, and some of the best laundries in existence are now to be found attached to army hospitals of the larger class. The importance of a good laundry to a hospital is by no means sufficiently appreciated. Neither are its dangers, if improperly placed. It would not be difficult to point to hospitals in which all the linen is washed within the hospital boundary, close under the ward windows, or in the basement of the hospital itself. I have even seen recent hospital plans in which it was proposed to place the laundry in this position, or even under the sick wards. A moment's consideration of what is likely to be the result to the atmosphere, and consequently to the sick of a hospital, by impregnating it with the steam of linen fouled by the excretions of a number of sick people, would surely be sufficient to put a stop to such errors in construction! May not some of the anomalous outbreaks of disease in hospitals be traced to this among other causes?

A great deal has been said about the communication of 'infectious' disease, both in civil and military hospitals, from patients' linen to washerwomen. The usual conclusion arrived at on such occasions, is that such and such a disease is 'very infectious;' *e.g.* I was lately told in a civil hospital that the washerwomen became infected with fever from the patients' linen. Have those who put forward this doctrine of inevitable 'infection' among washerwomen ever examined the process of washing, the appliances by which it is done, and the place where the women wash? If they will do so, they will very generally find a small, dark, wet, unventilated, and overcrowded little room or shed, in which there is hardly space to turn about—so full of steam loaded with organic matter that it is hardly possible to see across the room. Is it surprising that the linen is badly washed, that it is imperfectly dried, and that the washerwomen are poisoned by inhaling organic matter and foul air? An ordinary hospital wash-house is a very likely place indeed to contract disease in, but it supplies equal reason for demurring *in toto* to the doctrine that the occurrence is inevitable, or that the disease is to blame. Ignorance and mismanagement lie at the root of all such presumed cases of 'infection.' And it would better serve the cause of humanity if, instead of citing such facts—if they be facts—as illustrations that such and such a disease is infectious, people would reform these washing establishments and convert them into proper laundries, from which properly cleansed and prepared linen could be supplied to the sick, and in which the health of the servants could be preserved from injury.

Let hospital laundries be constructed in proper situations, with sufficient area and cubic space for each washer, with abundance of water, with proper means of drainage, and of ventilation for removing the vapour, and with properly-constructed drying and ironing rooms; it will be all the better for the sick, and we shall cease to hear of washerwomen 'catching' fever.

9. *Defective Accommodation for Nursing and Discipline.* —Want of simplicity of construction in not a few hospitals is destructive to discipline. Effectual and easy supervision is essential to proper care and nursing. And as everybody knows, a patient may often be saved by careful nursing when everything else will fail. It is at this point that the hospital architect may either facilitate or prevent recovery to the extent to which his plan renders nursing easy, or the reverse.

Every unneeded closet, scullery, sink, lobby, and staircase represents both a place which must be cleaned, which must take hands and time to clean, and a hiding or skulking place for patients or servants disposed to do wrong. And of such no hospital will ever be free. Every five minutes wasted upon cleaning what had better not have been there to be cleaned, is something taken from and lost by the sick.

But, on the other hand, there must be conveniences. From one of our most recently constructed hospitals, complaints have been made that there were no sufficient nursing conveniences, that nothing was at hand, that everything had to be sought. Where this is the case, the hospital administration must necessarily be both inefficient and costly.

There are four essential points of construction, as regards nursing and discipline, in which hospitals are generally deficient, from want of due consideration on the part of hospital architects. They are those points required to ensure :—1. Economy of attendance. 2. Ease of supervision. 3. Convenience as to number of sick in the same ward and on the same floor, so as to save extra attendants and unnecessary waste of time and strength on the stairs. 4. Sufficient accommodation for nurses so as to overlook their wards.

First. *Economy as to Attendance.*—I would rather not enumerate the instances where, often from the most various causes, one result arises, viz., that more time and care are given to passages, stairs, &c. &c., than to the sick. Extreme simplicity of construction and of detail is essential to obviate this. A convenient arrangement of lifts, and the laying of hot and cold water all over the building, economize attendance—certainly as much as one attendant to every thirty sick.

Secondly. *Ease of Supervision.*—The system of scouts, watch, alarm, is well understood in many wards where patients would be puzzled to give the things names. Some patients will know both things and names. Attendants require inspection as well as patients. Whatever system of hospital construction is adopted should provide for easy supervision at unexpected times. The Vincennes plan (No. 5) is better adapted for this than the Lariboisière plan (No. 4), inasmuch as there is a greater number of patients on the same level, and stairs are spared.

Third and Fourth. *Distribution of Sick in convenient numbers for Attendance, and Position of Nurses' Rooms.*—Four wards of ten patients each, taking the average of patients as in London, cannot be efficiently overlooked by one head nurse. Were it allowable to have forty patients in one ward, this number could be fully overlooked by one head nurse. She ought to have her room so placed that she can command her whole ward, day and night, from a window looking into the ward. This cannot be the case if she has four wards. If she has two, they ought to be built end to end, with her room placed between and looking into both wards.

Four wards of ten patients each cannot be attended by one night nurse, taking the average of London cases. Forty patients in one ward can be fully attended by one night nurse.

Small wards are indeed objectionable in working a hospital.

If we are to be guided, however, by the results of recent experience in hospital building, we shall probably come to the conclusion that, taking sanitary and administrative reasons together, thirty-two patients is a good ward-unit.

Let us see what we have done in our older military hospitals at home. The first thing that will strike any one in most of our old regimental hospitals is the extraordinary number of wards and of holes and corners, in comparison with the number of sick. In a hospital for a battalion 500 or 600 strong, you find eight or ten little bed-rooms, miscalled wards, a little kitchen—everything, in fact, on a little scale, like a collapsed hospital. How much more sensible would it be to have one, or at most two large wards for twenty-eight or thirty-two sick each, with a small 'casualty' ward! How much less the expense of erection and administration, how much easier the discipline and oversight, how much better the ventilation! In the recently erected military hospitals these errors have been avoided.

To return to large civil general hospitals. The 'casualty' wards, as they are called, for noisy or offensive cases are much better placed apart, with a completely appointed staff of their own, than attached one small ward to each larger one. Patients requiring much attention, whose condition fits them the most for the small wards, cannot be put there, because either they are more or less neglected or they unduly monopolize the service of the ward attendants. If convalescent patients are put into them, they are comparatively removed from inspection, and often play tricks there. If separate 'casualty' wards are provided as they ought to be, the small ward (often seen in French hospitals), at the end of the larger ward, is only an incubus.

10. *Defective Ward Furniture.* — Hospital bedsteads should always be of iron, the rest of the furniture of oak. Hair is the only material yet discovered fit for hospital mattresses. It is not hard nor cold. It is easily washed. It does not retain miasma. Straw has the advantage of being easily renewed, but it is not desirable. It is too hard and too cold not to render necessary the use of a blanket *under* the patient, which use is likely to encourage bed-sores. I speak from actual experience of the fatal effect of using the paillasse with patients much reduced. It may lower their vital energy beyond repair. Patients also say the straw feels to them 'like sticks,' and 'put their hands under them to move it.'

Among defective ward appurtenances, very liable to be undervalued in the results, may be enumerated eating, drinking, and washing vessels, of tin or any other metal, on account of their greater difficulty in being kept clean. It requires some care to ensure that any dark-coloured vessel is clean, and any means, by which extra care of this kind can be avoided in a hospital, are cheap and safe. Notwithstanding the greater amount of breakage and of expense, glass or earthenware is therefore best. Some kinds of tin vessels cannot by any amount of cleaning be freed from an unclean smell.

The more common and avoidable causes of hospital unhealthiness having been here enumerated, we will now discuss the principles on which hospitals should be constructed.

NOTE.—ON THE PROPORTION OF ATTENDANTS TO SICK IN DIFFERENT CLASSES OF HOSPITALS.

It is singular how little, even in civil hospitals, attention has been directed to the comparative cost of nursing in larger and smaller wards. In two civil hospitals in London, I found the annual cost of nursing each bed about one-third *more* in the one than in the other. It is true that the average number of constantly occupied beds was about one-third less in the former than in the latter hospital. But the difference of cost seems mainly attributable to the difference of the number of beds in each ward. And the efficiency of the nursing was certainly not less in the latter than in the former hospital.

In civil hospitals the proportion is 1 to every 7, generally of attendants to patients, but is mainly determined by the size of the ward:

In one of the hospitals alluded to, where there are quadruple wards of 44 or 48 patients, 11 or 12 in each compartment, the number of attendants is 7 to each quadruple ward. In exceptional cases extra night-nurses, sometimes extra day-nurses serve particular patients. The labour, both of cleaning and of night nursing, is much increased by the compartments being four, and separated by a large lobby.

In the other hospital the proportion of attendants to sick in the different wards was as follows:—

Patients.		Attendants.
22, 24	there were to each ward	1 Sister. 2 Nurses.
30	,,	1 Sister. 2 Nurses. 1 Scrubber.
34	,,	1 Sister. 3 Nurses.
40	,,	1 Sister. 3 Nurses. 1 Helper.

In the Lariboisière Hospital at Paris, where the wards hold 32 beds, 1 sister, 1 nurse, and 2 orderlies on the men's side, 1 sister, 2 nurses, and 1 orderly on the female side, serve the ward efficiently. In this hospital there are no lifts.

In all naval hospitals the regulation number of attendants is 1 to every 7 patients, or 2 attendants for each ward containing more than 7 patients and up to 14.

In military hospitals the regulation number of orderlies is 1 to every 10 patients, irrespective of the size of the wards.

The largest sized wards in the older class of military hospitals hold no more than 20 patients. But a ward of 20 patients cannot be efficiently served by two orderlies: nor (if the orderlies be men) with less than

$\frac{1}{2}$ Head Nurse—Female.
3 Orderlies.

And the other ward of this head nurse ought to be on the same floor.

The same number would quite as efficiently serve a ward of 32 patients, provided there be lifts and a supply of hot and cold water all over the building.

The army system of 1 orderly to 10 patients, with a number not exceeding 10 patients to a ward, is upset as immediately by one bad case among the 10, as by 9 to the 10.

Lifts and a supply of hot and cold water laid on all over the hospital, make, on an average, the difference of 1 attendant to every ward of 32 patients. And, other things being equal, it is certain that a ward with the appliances and without the extra attendant, will be better served than a ward without the appliances and with the extra attendant.

Another thing is certain. A nurse must not be a scrubber. And a scrubber cannot be a nurse.

Also, every night-nurse and every ward-attendant, scrubber included, must sleep and live and be entirely attached to the hospital which she serves. Otherwise it is obvious she will not serve it; she will serve some one else—probably her family at home. Also, every nurse on night duty must have regular night refreshment supplied her by the hospital.

One orderly should be trained to be the *frotteur* to each military ward. He should also be the porter to fetch and carry everything to and from the ward.

The following is an illustration of the cost of nursing in two military hospitals, one with large, the other with small wards:—

A ward of 9 sick would require 1 day and one night orderly, and a-third of a nurse (that is, a nurse could superintend three such wards).

A ward of 32 sick would require 2 day and 1 night orderlies and 1 nurse = 4 persons in all.

Or if two such wards were on one floor, 1 nurse could serve both.

We cannot count the cost of orderlies and nurses, including lodging, rations, wages, at less than 50*l.* a year, which when capitalized at 3 per cent. (33 years' purchase), would amount to 1650*l.* for each.

A ward of 9 sick would cost in nursing 1650*l.* × $2\frac{1}{3}$ = 3850*l.* or 427*l.* 15*s.* 6*d.* per bed.

A ward of 32 sick would cost for nursing, in perpetuity, 1650*l.* × 4 = 6600*l.* = 220*l.* per bed.

[One nurse to each ward is here allowed.]

The cost of the two plans relatively for a hospital of 1000 sick would stand thus:—

Wards with 9 beds =	£427,775
Wards with 30 beds =	220,000
Capitalized difference of cost in favour of large wards	£207,775

Suppose there be 25 sick to a ward, the cost would stand thus:—

For each ward of 25 sick, 3 orderlies, at 1650*l.* . . =	£4950
If two such are built in line close to each other, with the nurse's room between them, one nurse could superintend both wards, or half a nurse to a ward. The cost would be for the ward . . .	825
	£5775

Or cost for each bed $\frac{5775}{25}$ = £231

The comparative cost of wards with 9 beds and 25 beds would stand thus for 1000 sick:—

Wards with 9 beds	£427,775
Wards with 25 beds	231,000
Saving	£196,775

III.

PRINCIPLES OF HOSPITAL CONSTRUCTION.

THE first principle of hospital construction is to divide the sick among separate pavilions. By a hospital pavilion is meant a detached block of building, capable of containing the largest number of beds that can be placed safely in it, together with suitable nurses' rooms, ward sculleries, lavatories, baths, water-closets, all complete, proportioned to the number of sick, and quite unconnected with any other pavilions of which the hospital may consist, or with the general administrative offices, except by light airy passages or corridors. A pavilion is indeed a separate detached hospital, which has, or ought to have, as little connexion in its ventilation with any other part of the hospital, as if it were really a separate establishment miles away. The essential feature of the pavilion construction is that of breaking up hospitals of any size into a number of separate detached parts, having a common administration, but nothing else in common. And the object sought is that the atmosphere of no one pavilion or ward should diffuse itself to any other pavilion or ward, but should escape into the open air as speedily as possible, while its place is supplied by the purest obtainable air from the outside.

The question of a general hospital plan resolves itself, first of all, into obtaining the most healthy structure of the pavilion; and second, into arranging all the pavilions in the way best suited to obtain free external ventilation, plenty of light on all sides, and convenient means of communication. To realize these advantages, pavilions may be placed side by side, or in line.

The arrangement of pavilions side by side should be adopted for hospitals of above 120 beds; the arrangement in line is most suitable for small hospitals with fewer than 120 beds. In the larger class of hospitals the arrangement of pavilions side by side diminishes the distance to be traversed from block to block, and thus materially facilitates the administration.

Besides this, it allows covered communications to be kept up between all parts of the hospital, without interfering with the lighting or ventilation of the wards.

The distance between the blocks should not be less than double the height of the blocks. This rule is specially applicable to English climates, in which it is necessary to preserve as much space as possible for sunshine. A greater distance would be better; but this would involve a greater cost for land, and a greater distance to be traversed by the hospital staff. Generally the distance between the pavilions should be greater than twice their height in low confined localities, where there is not a free external movement of the air. If the wards are raised on basements, the rule as to distance should apply only to the height of the pavilion from the floor of the ground-floor ward. In very close positions it is difficult to say what distance will be found sufficient for free ventilation. Such localities are precisely those where no hospitals should be built.

The first thing, however, is to determine the best construction for a pavilion, and in doing this, the following principles require to be kept in view:—

1. Number of Floors in a Pavilion.

There should not be more than two floors of wards to the block.

The most healthy hospitals have been those on one floor only; and this because they require less scientific knowledge and practical care in ventilation. If another floor is added, a community of ventilation exists between the ward below and the ward above by the common staircase, and by filtration of air upwards through the floor. The risk from this can be diminished by constant care in the use of doors and windows, and by introducing impervious floors. But, unfortunately, systematic care in these matters is not to be looked for, especially that constant supervision necessary to keep the ventilation of three or more floors of wards quite independent of each other. [Who ever sees this, even in a private house, where there is an invalid?] And hence there is a strong conviction in the minds of careful hospital physicians, surgeons, and nurses, that patients do not recover so well on upper floors. And there are instances in which the mortality of patients on upper floors has been higher than that of the floors below. Moreover, a *sick population* requires more surface for health than a healthy population. And it is clear that, if patients are placed on three floors instead of on two, the surface overcrowding is increased by one-third, unless the distance between the pavilions is increased in a corresponding ratio. But the general administration of lofty hospitals is also far more difficult and fatiguing than of those of moderate height: any increase of distance between the pavilions will add to the difficulty, and both difficulty and fatigue are very important considerations for efficiency and economy in this branch.

To sum up. Hospitals on one floor require least care;

hospitals on two floors can be kept healthy with moderate average care and intelligence. Beyond this, care, intelligence, and fatigue, such as are rarely likely to be bestowed, are essential to maintain a moderate average amount of health, among either wards or nurses. Nobody but those who have had to do with running up and down lofty hospitals can have any idea of the waste of time and strength it entails. The objection usually urged is that hospitals in two floors cost more than in three or more floors. But I submit that this is not the question before us, which is how to construct a hospital with the requisite facilities for ventilation, administration, nursing, and health.

The mode of construction in hospitals is, it is presumed, to be determined by that which is best for the recovery of the sick. If any other consideration is taken, such or such a per-centage of mortality is to be sacrificed to that other consideration.

But it so happens that the safest for the sick is in reality the most economical mode of construction.

2. Number of Wards to a Floor.

If the pavilions are single, *i.e.*, if each staircase gives access to the end of the pavilion, as in the Lariboisière and Lisbon plans, Nos. 4 and 11, there should be only one ward on each floor. The pavilion should never be divided so that a second ward or wards is placed beyond the first, to be reached by passing through the first. The reason is that the floor, however divided by cross-walls, can never be other than a single ward. The cross-walls only obstruct the ventilation. If the doors are accidentally left open, the foul air in one ward passes into the next, and the greatest improvement in ventilation would be to pull down all the partitions and throw the pavilion open from end to end, so as to have only one ward on the floor.

To illustrate the meaning of this, here is a plan (fig. 11) of one wing of the Hôpital Necker at Paris, in which it will be seen that an excellently constructed ward, with windows on all sides, is cut up by partitions into four wards. If the partitions were removed, one cannot fail to see that the ventilation would be better, but in this case the ward would be too large.

FIG. 11.

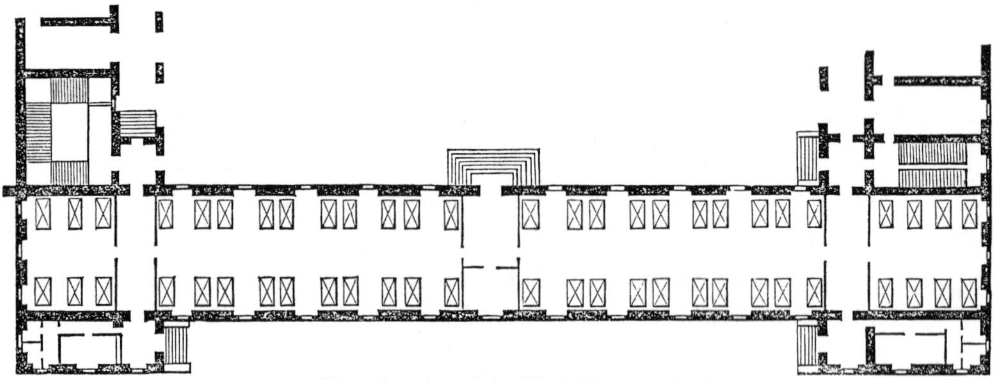

Plan of a wing of the Hôpital Necker, Paris.

If the pavilions are double, *i.e.*, if each staircase gives access to a ward right and left off the staircase, as in the Herbert Hospital No. 6 and in the Regimental Hospital plans, figs. 20, 21, provided the staircase be of spacious size, and thoroughly ventilated sides and top, two wards may be placed on each floor with safety; and with this great advantage, that administration, nursing, and discipline are all facilitated, while expense in construction is saved. One staircase does the work of two for the same number of sick; or rather, one staircase answers for double the number of sick.

3. Size of Wards, Pavilions, and Hospitals.

The question, what is the best number of beds in a ward? has been but little considered in England in regard either to health, economy, or efficiency of service. The more beds in one ward, the fewer the attendants necessary in proportion, and, within a certain limit, the greater the facility of supervision. But the sanitary necessities of cubic space per bed, &c., impose the limit. After we have attained a certain number of beds per ward, the height of the ward becomes too little for its other dimensions. The ventilation becomes impeded, a circumstance which can only be guarded against by making the ward higher than necessary. Additional cubic space has thus to be given; and the construction ceases to be economical. Without the most perfect ventilation, there is always more danger of effluvia being driven by a draught till it accumulates in one part of a very large ward, as was the case in the long corridors of Scutari. Besides which, you may make your ward too large for the chief attendant to overlook the whole at a glance, which he and still more *she* ought to be able to do. And you would have to double your supervision.*

Wards of a small size are decidedly objectionable, because unfavourable to discipline, inasmuch as a small number, when placed together in the same ward, more readily associate together for any breach of discipline than a larger number.

It has been proved by experience that the presence of head nurses, whether male or female, one to each ward, is

---

* See Note to Section II., on the relation which the size and arrangement of wards bears to the question of nursing and supervision.

essential to discipline, and a sufficient number of such nurses cannot be allotted in smaller wards. One head nurse can easily overlook all the patients in one large ward. In four small ones it is almost impossible.

The best size of wards for ensuring the two conditions of health and facility of administration and discipline, is from 20 to 32 sick.

Wards smaller than of 20 beds multiply both the attendance, unnecessarily, and the corners, unfavourably for ventilation, in proportion to the number of patients. Wards larger than of 32 beds are undesirable, because they require a greater height of ceiling, and are hence more costly in construction and difficult to ventilate.

In the event of a death taking place in the ward, the survivors, when they are few in number, are far more likely to be affected by it than a larger number.

Wards, again, much smaller than of 20 beds are more difficult to ventilate by natural means alone. A certain amount of space is requisite for diffusion, in order to secure perfect natural ventilation.

Wards of a moderate size, like those indicated, are better for the purposes of ventilation than wards half the size; and are less subject to a hospital atmosphere than wards of double the size.

Where clinical instruction is intended, to admit even a class of six students into a ward of 12 sick is increasing the population in the cubic space by one-half. There is more than twice the room proportionally for students, in a ward of double the size. On the other hand, if the number of students be very large, a ward of 20 patients, it must be at once admitted, is too small. The size of the ward must be increased, and with it its height and its cubic space; for, be it remembered, the whole of the proportions of the ward, not only its length, must increase with its number of beds; for, if the ward be very long, in proportion to its height and breadth, it becomes not a ward but a corridor, and all corridors are objectionable for sick, because it is impossible to ventilate them safely; because, as already stated, in admitting air, the effluvia may be driven from one end and be accumulated at the opposite end faster than they can be taken out. The right proportion is a fixed one.

As to the size of the pavilion. If the pavilion be single and in two floors, it will of course contain under one roof no more than the sick of the two wards, *i.e.*, of 32 beds each, or 64 in all. With double pavilions and intervening staircases, the number would be double. *i.e.*, 128 beds. Where small wards for special cases are required, they can always, as a point of construction in small hospitals, be attached to the pavilion, which would add a few more beds to the number which can be accommodated under a single roof. In good existing examples small wards have been thrown out separately from the staircase.

Guided by these considerations, a hospital, consisting of two end to end pavilions, such as would be required for a county establishment receiving a small number of sick, would contain, say, 68 beds under one roof, *i.e.*, 32 beds in each of the large wards, and two beds in each of the small wards. A double pavilion hospital would contain double that number. It would thus be safe, so far as plan is concerned, to construct a large hospital of any administrable size of separate double pavilions, each containing, say, 136 beds. But in large hospitals the smaller class of special wards should always be grouped together, and completely separated from the other wards, because they are intended to contain either the most dangerous and important cases, or noisy cases, or cases with offensive discharges, which it is always safest to remove from the general wards; besides, small wards require, if possible, purer air than larger wards, and therefore more care in construction; and in order to insure those cases which really require most nursing from neglect, they should always be placed under a completely appointed staff of their own: and *not* attached, one to each large ward, which renders proper attendance extremely difficult.

The next point is to determine what ought to be the size of a hospital; in other words, how many beds it can contain with safety. But from what has been said, it will be observed that this question resolves itself into the previous one, viz., what should be the size of each hospital pavilion? because, if a pavilion of healthy construction is obtained, it is evident that the only limit to the size of the hospital will be an administrative one. A hospital may be constructed for any number of sick, until a point is arrived at, when some portion of the administrative arrangements, material or personal, has to be provided in duplicate. Any further extension beyond this ceases to be economical.

Considering each pavilion as a separate unit in the hospital construction, any number of single or double pavilions could be put together up to accommodation for, say, 1000 beds, beyond which it would be difficult, if not impracticable, to have good administration with one set of officers. It is to be hoped, however, that few hospitals will ever be built for such a number now-a-days. The fewer hospitals required, and the smaller their number of sick, the better will it be for civilization. All I submit is, that the pavilion construction may, not should, be safely used up to this extent.

4. Space and Area to the Bed.

Having determined the number of beds per ward, the next point is to ascertain what amount of cubic space should be given to each patient. There is scarcely a point of hospital construction in which there has been so much error as in this. The chief element in the question, and that one which has been very generally overlooked, is the superficial area per bed. If it be—as it is—an essential condition to the healthy state of a hospital that there should be ample facility for the air moving around and in the immediate vicinity of the sick, it is quite clear that, if the beds are placed as close as they can stand, it matters very little whether you give your patient 1000 cubic feet or 20,000 cubic feet. To show the importance of this, it may be sufficient to state that, if a large building, say a church, be selected for a war hospital, on account of its spacious, light, cheerful aspect, if it be measured to ascertain its cubic contents, its height being no more than 60 feet, in such a building the very liberal war hospital allowance of 1200 cubic feet per bed would render it necessary to place the beds on the floor so close together that not even a pathway would be left between them. Has not this, in times past, been one cause of the frightful mortality in these hospitals? In some splendid new hospitals in India, where they give above 1000 cubic feet per bed, the superficial area for each patient is only 24 square feet. But then the architect has made such a spacious ward, no less than 42 feet high (!), that it is supposed to make amends.

Let us inquire what is the smallest amount of superficial area we can do with. Hospital beds are generally from 3 feet to 3 feet 6 inches wide, and 6 feet 3 inches long, the bed space being increased to 7 feet by the bed being a little removed from the wall.

The mere surface required to hold the bed is hence from 21 square feet to 24½ square feet. It is quite clear that, whatever surface area is required for ventilation, administration, or for clinical instruction, must be in excess of this amount. There should be space sufficient between the sides of adjacent beds to avoid stagnation of air altogether. There should also be room for free movement of three or four persons, for the use of a night-chair, without annoying the next patient, and also for a portable bath, when required. The distance from foot to foot of opposite beds should be sufficient to afford space for a movable dresser or table, benches on either side, and easy passage-way. In a well-constructed civil hospital in England, occupying a healthy airy position, it cannot be said that 80 square feet *besides* the bed space, are too much. In round numbers, the superficial area per bed should be not less than 100 square feet.

Wards for the numbers of beds already given need not be higher than 15 feet, which would allow 1500 cubic feet per bed. This ought to be quite sufficient in a well-constructed hospital in a healthy position, and for the average class of cases received into civil hospitals. For small wards, however, neither this superficial area nor cubic space would be sufficient. In these wards the space per bed should be, as near as may be, 2500 cubic feet; and this partly from the more severe nature of the cases, partly from the greater difficulty of ventilating this class of wards.

If, however, a hospital is built in the centre of a large city, where pure air is not to be had, or in a locality where the circulation of air outside is deficient, it is hard to say what amount of space would make the building healthy. We know of hospitals where 2000 cubic feet per patient are not sufficient to make the wards safe. But these hospitals should not be there at all.

A good proportion for a ward of 20 patients would be 80 feet long, 25 (or 26) feet wide, and 16 (or 15) feet high. This would give 1600 (or 1560) cubic feet to each bed. It would give 11 (or 12) feet between foot and foot, which is not too much where there is a clinical school. It would give an average of 16 feet to each 2 beds in width.

Half the sick are supposed to be on each side the ward.

5. Number of Beds to a Window.

One window at least should be allotted for every two beds; the window to be not less than 4 feet 8 inches wide, the sill within 2 or 3 feet of the floor, so that the patient can see out, and up to within a foot of the ceiling.

The pair of beds should have the width of the window between them on one side, and in the wall space between the windows the beds should be not less than 3 feet apart. With a very bad fever case, I would leave one bed empty, for the sake of isolating the patient. Miasma may be said, roughly speaking, to diminish as the square of the distance. With good ventilation, it is not found to extend much beyond 3 feet from the patient; although miasma from the excretions may extend a considerably greater distance.

Windows are to be placed opposite each other, and to be either double or filled with plate glass; the former would be preferable, as affording the opportunity of indirect ventilation in all weather. But attendants find them too difficult to manage and to clean, so as to be cheerful.

Windows opening as at Middlesex and Guy's Hospitals, in three or more parts, with an iron casting outside, to prevent a delirious patient from throwing himself out, are the best form of plate-glass window.

No part of the ward ought to be dark. This is of the

utmost importance, in many cases. The light can always be modified for individual patients. But even for such patients to have light in the ward is not the less important.

There are three reasons for this multiplicity of windows :—

1. Light.
2. Ventilation.
3. To enable patients to read in bed.

The necessity of light for health is established by scientific inquiry and experience. The proportion of window space to cubic space in a room, but especially in a ward, is a point of the first importance. It has been lost sight of in English architecture, owing to the unfortunate window-tax, which has left its legacy in giving us a far smaller proportion of light than in French houses. In huts the proportion of window space to cubic space is far greater than in buildings. One main cause of the unhealthiness of large numbers of men congregated in one large building, even with sufficient cubic space, is the disproportionately small window space.

For the same purpose of ensuring a sufficiency of light, the walls should always be light coloured, excepting perhaps for some few cases of ophthalmia.

6. Material for Walls and Ceilings of Wards.

One of the most difficult points in ward construction is to find a good material for walls and ceilings.

An impervious material capable of receiving a polish on a white or tinted surface would make the best lining for a hospital ward. What is wanted is such a surface as can be washed frequently with soap and water, without its being absorbed into the substance, and dried with towels, so as not to interfere with the current use of the ward. Parian cement is the nearest approach to a good material for this purpose hitherto discovered. But the polish is rather costly. And what is of more consequence, the manufacture has not yet reached such a point of perfection as to afford a surface of one uniform colour. Even the best becomes blotchy after a short time, and is liable to crack, especially when applied to ceilings. If manufacturers wish to bring this substance into general use for Hospitals, they must improve the material until the cement can be applied over any required extent of wall, and retain an uniform texture, colour, and polish. Various silicated surfaces have recently been introduced for walls. Some of these are worthy of trial—always bearing in mind that a good colour, and not a dull dirty one, is necessary in all sick wards. It is possible that a sufficiently good surface might be obtained by applying some of the better class of light-coloured paints in repeated coats over unpolished Parian, and then varnishing and polishing the surface.

All the woodwork should be painted and varnished in such a way as to admit of ready washing and drying. But the best material is polished or varnished wainscot oak. It is the cleanest, most durable, and most satisfactory in use.

7. Ward Floors.

The materials used for floors may be oak wood, pine wood, or tiles.

Oak wood, well seasoned, is the best. No sawdust or other organic matter capable of rotting should be placed underneath the floor. Concrete, or some similar indestructible substance, would be the best for the purpose. The floors at the new Herbert Hospital, Woolwich, are formed of concrete, supported by wrought-iron joists, over which the wood is laid. They are consequently fire-proof, as all hospital floors ought to be.

The reason for using oak wood is, that it is capable of absorbing but a very small quantity of water. And it is very desirable to diminish even that capability, by saturating it with beeswax and turpentine. Beeswax is an inalterable substance. This floor should be cleaned like the French *parquet*, by *frottage*.

A hospital floor should never be scoured. A very good hospital floor is that used at Berlin, which is oiled, lackered, and polished so as to resemble French polish. It is wet-rubbed and dry-rubbed every morning, which removes the dust. Its only objection is want of durability.

Both processes render the floor non-absorbent—both processes do away with the necessity of scouring altogether. The French floor *stands* the most wear and tear, but must be cleaned by a *frotteur*, which cleaning is more laborious than scrubbing, and does not remove the dust. The Prussian floor requires re-preparing every three years. But the wet and dry rubbing, or process of cleaning, is far less laborious than either *frottage* or scrubbing, and completely removes the dust, and freshens the ward in the morning. By either process the sick would gain much in England. The Berlin flooring is by no means perfect, on account of this deficient durability of surface, and might be improved. Practically, with care, a well-laid oak floor, with a good bees-waxed surface, can always be kept clean by rubbing ; but the means of producing a really good impervious polished surface, with little labour, have yet to be discovered.

The joints of the flooring must be fitted well together, and cemented with any impervious substance. The object is, of course, to prevent any water from entering the floor.

Impervious, non-absorbent cement or composition would make a capital floor, used as it is in Italian houses. But, on account of its great conducting power, it would be necessary to furnish each patient with a pair of list shoes, and a small bedside carpet. Flooring of this kind, or of tiles, is better suited for a warm than for a cold climate.

The stairs and landings should be of stone. The corridors should be floored with diamond-shaped flags or tiles, which stand better than those laid in the usual manner. The terraces over the corridors might be either covered with asphalte or glazed tile, to admit of convalescents walking on them, and of patients in bed being wheeled out on them.

8. Sisters' Rooms and Sculleries.

There should be a "sister's" room on one side of the ward door. This room must have superficial area enough to be the nurse's bed-room and living-room, being, as she is, the head nurse or "sister" of her ward, and therefore in immediate command of it, night and day. A scullery should be attached to each ward, on the side of the passage opposite the nurse's room. The scullery must be supplied with complete, efficient, simple apparatus for its various purposes, places for washing up and cleaning, and for *ward* cookery, so that the "sister" can warm the drinks, prepare fomentations, &c., without jostling the nurses or orderlies who are washing up. The best sink for a scullery is the new white porcelain sink recently introduced, with hot and cold water laid on. Care must be taken that the waste-pipe has no direct communication with a closed drain, otherwise foul air is certain to find its way into the hospital. The scullery should be large enough for the assistant nurses to sit in to have their meals comfortably.

9. Bath Rooms and Lavatories.

Every hospital of any large size should have a separate bathing establishment at a convenient distance from the pavilions, but connected by the corridors.

The walls of the bath house should be of white tiles, or cement, the floors of wood. The apartments should be suitably ventilated and warmed. They should contain hot and cold water baths, sulphureous water, hot air, medicated and vapour baths, shower baths, and douche.

There should also be a small bath room with one fixed bath of white glazed terra-cotta supplied with hot and cold water adjoining each large ward. Terra-cotta has the advantage of retaining the heat longer than almost any other material, and of being always cleanly.

A lavatory table with a row of sunk white porcelain basins, with outlet-tubes and plugs, each basin supplied with hot and cold water, should be placed in the same compartment as the bath, but separated from it by a partition and door. It is a common mistake to place these lavatory basins too near each other to be used conveniently by men-patients standing abreast.

There should also be room for a portable bath to each ward, with a hot and cold water supply at hand, and means of running off the bath water after it has been used.

10. Water-closets and Sinks.

The water-closets should be placed at the end of the ward opposite the entrance, and separated by a lighted and ventilated lobby. They should never be against the inner wall, but always against the outer wall of the compartment in which they are placed. They should be of the best construction. A syphon water-closet of a hemispherical shape, *never of a conical shape*, and abundantly supplied with water to flush it out with a large forcible stream, is by far the best contrivance of the kind for a hospital. The cost of water is a bagatelle in comparison with the advantages. The sink for ward slops, bed-pans, expectoration cups, &c., which should have a compartment of its own, adjoining the water-closet, should be a high, large, deep, round, pierced basin of earthenware, above a *large* hole, with a cock extending far enough over the sink for the stream of water to fall directly into the vessel to be cleansed. This is far preferable to the usual oblong sink. The scullery sink is, of course, to be entirely separate, and for entirely different purposes from this. The only way to ensure dryness and cleanliness in the compartments where the water-closets and lavatory accommodation are placed, is to cover the walls with white glazed tile, enamelled slate, or cement.

It is, perhaps, hardly necessary to say that there must be private water-closets for the hospital officers, for the nurses, who should not be compelled to use those of the patients, (and, of course, *never* those in the men's wards), also water-closets for the patients when not in their wards. Patients should not be allowed to use the ward ones, except when confined to their wards.

All these water-closets fall under the same rules of health as those laid down.

As the arrangement of this part of a hospital—viz., lavatories, water-closets, &c.—is one of primary importance, a measured plan of the most improved arrangement of ward offices, such as has been introduced into recent military hospitals (fig. 12), is given next page.

FIG. 12.

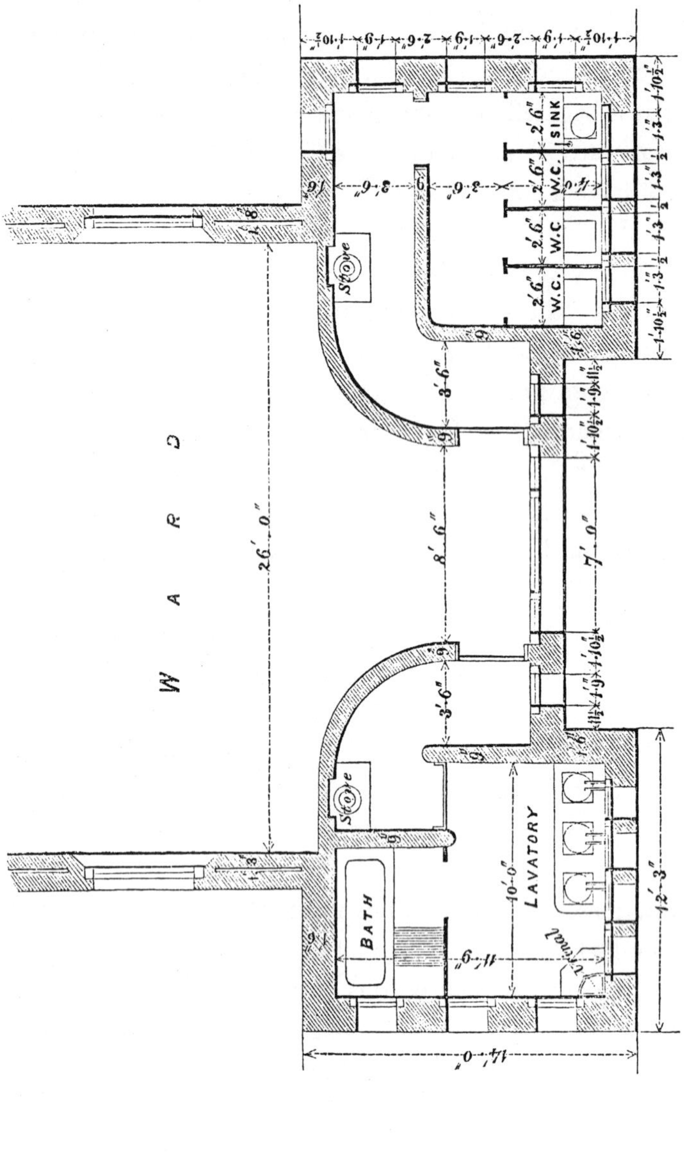

Plan of Lavatory, Baths, and Water-closets for Hospital Wards.

11. Ventilation of Wards.

The doors, windows, and fire-places should be the chief means of ventilation for properly constructed wards. If a hospital must be ventilated artificially, it betrays a defect of original construction which no artificial ventilation can compensate; it is an expensive and inefficient means of doing that which can be done cheaply and efficiently by constructing your building so as to admit the open air around.

In countries where fuel is dear and cold severe, the problem complicates itself, because it is supposed to require a smaller consumption of fuel to warm the fresh air as you admit it.

Artificial ventilation means the use of some machine or method whereby air is drawn from without—sometimes, it is to be feared, without due care whence it comes—bringing the air into forcible contact with heated surfaces, generally of hot water vessels, and then introducing it into the ward for the use of the sick. The foul air is either expelled or drawn out of the ward by some mechanical means, and the fresh (if it is ever fresh) warmed air takes its place. In certain Parisian hospitals where this system is applied, the fresh warmed air enters the ward by pedestals down the centre; and the foul air is extracted by openings close to the floor between the beds—the presumption being that the foul air is in this way taken off before mingling with the general air of the ward.

It is a fact that one hospital at least in which this system is in full operation yields, notwithstanding its otherwise excellent construction, a very high death-rate among its inmates. English physicians and surgeons, who have examined this hospital, concur in stating that the ward atmosphere is by no means so pure as it is in a London hospital. These facts have led to considerable discussion, which it is necessary to notice. Here we have one of the best constructed hospitals in existence, professing to afford to each of its beds from 2500 to 5000 cubic feet of "fresh warmed air" per hour, introduced, and the foul air removed, in accordance with strictly correct scientific principle—and yet here is the result.

It strikes one, on examining this process, that it is not in accordance with Nature's method of providing fresh air. She affords air, both to sick and healthy, of varying temperature at different hours of the day, night, and season—always apportioning the quantity of moisture to the temperature, providing continuous free movement everywhere, and warming not by warm water in iron pipes, but by radiant heat. We all know how necessary the variations of weather, temperature, season, are for maintaining health in healthy people.

Have we any right to assume that the natural law is different in sickness? In looking solely at combined warming and ventilation, to ensure to the sick a certain amount of air at 60°, paid for by contract, are we acting in accordance with physiological law? Is it a likely way to enable the constitution to rally under serious disease or injury, to under-cook all the patients, day and night, during all the time they are in hospital, at one fixed temperature? I believe not. On the contrary, I am strongly of opinion, I would go farther and say, I am certain that the atmospheric hygiene of the sick room ought not to be very different from the atmospheric hygiene of a healthy house. Continuous change of the atmosphere of a sick ward to a far greater extent than would pay a contractor to maintain, together with the usual variations of temperature and moisture given by nature in the external atmosphere, are elements as essential as any other elements to the rapid recovery of the sick in most cases.

The best way to cure these beautiful but unhealthy buildings would be to remove the warming and ventilating apparatus, to put in chimneys, with good radiating open fire-places, and to trust to their magnificent supply of windows for fresh air.* [This is done in Russia, where it is far colder than at Paris.] The administration would complain of the additional cost of fuel. But I would reply, you must consider how much you prolong the stay of sick in your hospital, and what per-centage of recoveries you prevent or delay, by this combined warming and ventilation. It does not matter what the present saving may appear to be; the object of your magnificent charities, perhaps the finest in the world, is to recover the largest number of sick in the shortest possible time. It is to be feared the statistics show that this end is not obtained.

Natural ventilation and open radiating fire-places are the only suitable means of renewing and warming the air in hospitals. Whenever the weather permits of it, the windows of every sick-ward should be more or less open. During cold, boisterous weather, and at night, a sufficient renewal of the air can always be obtained, even if the windows cannot be opened, by the method recently introduced into English military hospitals of carrying up a few air-shafts from the ceilings of the wards to above the roof, and allowing fresh air to enter by

* Why do not all learn the lesson taught by the experience of the invasions of France in 1814-15? At that date the hospital administration of Paris, not knowing where to receive the sick and wounded, fitted up three of the unfinished "*Abattoirs*" for 6000 patients,—several of the buildings fortunately had neither doors nor windows, and had the wind blowing through them. The mortality was one-half among the patients in the "Abattoirs" of what it was in the ordinary hospital establishments.—*Husson. Etude*, p. 39.

means of Sherringham's ventilators at the top of the ward walls, close to the ceilings. No other system is required but this, and it costs little or nothing; besides which, it takes advantage of the natural laws of varying temperature and moisture.

Fig. 13 shows the ventilating arrangements for a ward in plan. A foul-air shaft is carried up in each alternate wall-space between the windows, and a Sherringham's ventilating inlet is placed close to the ceiling in each alternate wall-space opposite the shaft.

FIG. 13.

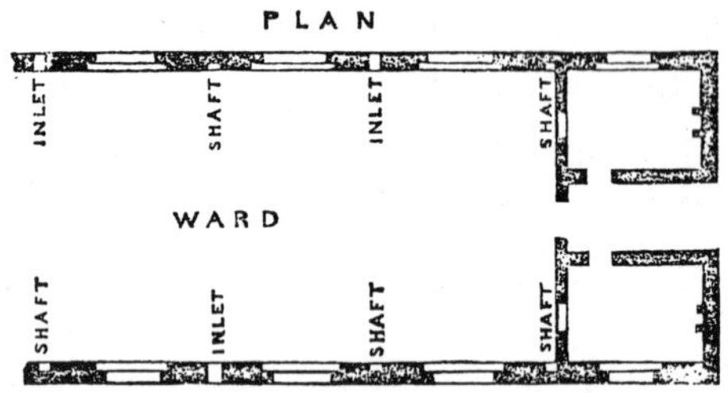

Plan of Ward Ventilation, showing the position of Shafts and Inlets.

Fig. 14 gives a section of the shafts and inlets. The shafts are louvred at the lower ends to prevent chance down-draughts falling on the beds.

Fig. 15 is Sherringham's ventilator used as an inlet. It can be opened or shut by a weighted cord to regulate the amount of fresh air.

If with these simple means, including windows, attendants cannot be trained to keep the rooms ventilated without draughts, there is a defect of intelligence, and attendance on the sick is not their calling.

There should be one or more open fire-places, according to the size of the ward, but lofty, so that the throat of the chimney shall be above the patient's head and bed.

Fig. 14.

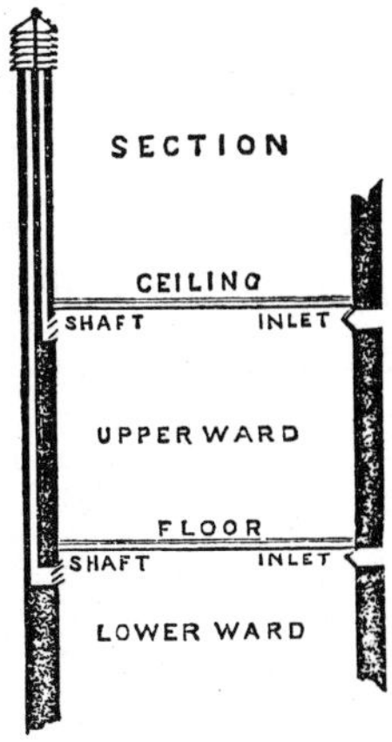

Section of Ward Ventilation.

Fig. 15.

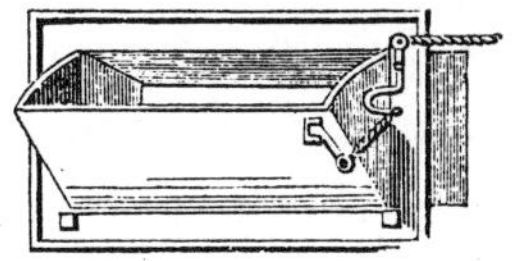

Sherringham's Ventilating Inlet.

The chimney is indispensable as a ventilating shaft; the fire sets it acting; it takes the air from the ward so successfully that, as has been proved by direct experiment, a single chimney will, in certain states of the wind, remove 60,000 cubic feet of air in an hour, or as much as the French contract system allows for 24 patients.

12. Ward Furniture.

White window-curtains are used in some French hospitals, not tó exclude the light, but to look cheerful. In most French hospitals, and in some in this country, the beds have curtains. They are not necessary. They interrupt ventilation and entail additional cost in washing. Where seclusion of a patient is required, a low moveable screen, not higher than the patient's head when he is sitting up in bed, is far preferable.

Oak furniture should be supplied for wards. There

should be a light chair for each bed, two or three spare arm-chairs for patients who get up for the first time to sit at the ward fire; there should be a small open bed-table for each bed; two or more tables or moveable dressers down the centre of the ward, according to its dimensions; one or two forms with backs would be found very useful. In some hospitals the allowance of furniture is more liberal, but the less ward furniture, speaking generally, the better. The use of glass or earthenware for all eating, drinking, and washing vessels is recommended from its great superiority in cleanliness, and in saving time and labour in cleaning. Tin vessels of certain kinds cannot, by any amount of cleaning, be freed from smell.

13. Bedding.

No bedding but the hair mattress has yet been discovered that is fit for hospitals. Hair is indestructible. It does not readily retain miasma. And, if it does, heat easily disinfects it. It may be washed. It is not hard to the patient. It saves the objectionable use of a blanket UNDER the patient. There have been repeated objections to the use of horsehair on account of the current expense. But this, under careful administration, is much less than is generally supposed. From special inquiries, I find that, allowing 5 per cent. for deterioration, the cost would stand as follows:—

	Per Bed per Annum.
Cleaning and remaking,	$2\frac{1}{4}d.$ to $2\frac{1}{2}d.$
Loss of hair . . .	$1\frac{1}{2}d.$ to $2d.$
Interest at 5 per cent.	$2s.$
Total	$2s.\ 3\frac{3}{4}d.$ to $2s.\ 4\frac{1}{2}d.$

Straw paillasses, as already stated, are inadmissible. They

are cold ; and, in some cases, the abstraction of heat from the spine lowers the patient's vital energy to a degree which does not leave him a chance of recovery. I am of opinion that the loss of life must have been great during the war from laying our patients on paillasses, which were either placed on wooden divans, or on the flagged corridors, with only a mat between.

All bedsteads for hospital use should be of wrought iron, frequently painted of a light cheerful colour. This costs little; and yet it has a far greater influence on the general appearance and comfort of a hospital ward than most people are aware of. Just in proportion to the discrepancy between the spacious, cheerful ward and its shabby dirty-looking furnishing, is the air of general discomfort which it presents. A head shelf to the bed is useful. The French military hospital bedsteads have one at the feet too.

Sacking bottoms are preferable to iron bottoms, which are stated to harbour vermin between the interlacings, and it is said that the edges of the iron bands cut the bed-ticks. The Rheocline open iron springs, like snakes sitting on their bottom ring, make the easiest, best ventilated, freshest bed I know; save your bed-ticks by sewing a sacking under them. Some cases, like compound fractures, require a firm bottom to the bed for the splints and apparatus to rest upon. A wooden frame or such like may be made to fit the bedstead for such cases.

Every hospital should have dropsy and surgical bedsteads for raising a patient when he cannot be moved, for inclining him at a certain angle, &c., also water and air beds. For many purposes different forms of new spring bedsteads will be found very useful.

14. Water Supply.

One of the most essential sanitary provisions for a hospital is an abundant supply of pure, soft water. The obtaining of such a supply pre-supposes a careful examination of the sources, and a chemical analysis, both quantitative and qualitative. It has frequently happened, especially in warm climates, that waters of a most impure character, containing poisonous amounts of dissolved organic matter, have been used for sick, without suspicion that the diarrhœa or dysentery of which they were dying was nothing more than a *water disease*. Absence of colour, taste, and smell is no criterion of sufficient purity; for some of the most impure waters are often the most agreeable; as, *e.g.*, the water drawn from wells supplied by filtration through old grave-yards is often clear, bright, and sparkling, from being charged with carbonic acid derived from human remains in the soil; and during an epidemic, poisonous.

Hard water, containing sulphates or carbonates, is unfit for most hospital purposes—especially so for dressing wounds. Filtered rain water is generally the best for this purpose. In small hospitals, either spring or well-water should be selected after analysis, and if found to be hard, the roof water should be stored for surgical purposes. In large hospitals, where no other than a *hard* water supply can be obtained, it will be possible to soften the water by the lime process. But in large hospitals, where engine power is used, there is often much waste steam which can be usefully condensed for soft water. Of course, for all pharmaceutical purposes, the softer the water the better: and the same rule holds for the cooking, especially of vegetables.

Having obtained the best available water source, all the

water required for ordinary ward purposes should be laid on at pressure, hot and cold, all over the building, for sinks, ablution basins and baths; but never from a cistern within the hospital. This would be to expose the water to impurity, and the hospital to damp.

The consumption of water for an English hospital, including, besides patients, all its officers and servants (who may be roughly estimated as 150 for 500 patients), is on an average of 25 gallons for each person per day. This includes baths, brewing, washing the pavements, but *not* laundry work, farther than the necessary wringing out of soiled sheets, &c., before sending to the laundry. Of this amount two-thirds at least should be soft water for personal use—one-third being for domestic purposes may be hard. In the laboratory of a hospital of this size, the steam boiler will supply 500 gallons of condensed water per day, to be used for all mixtures, decoctions, infusions, &c., and collected in iron or slate cisterns for the purpose. One gallon of soft water per patient per day is thus on an average required for the pharmacy. I may just allude to the difficulty, if you have one tap of soft water and one of hard, of making sure that the attendants never use the hard for soft-water purposes.

There should be convenient means in or close to the wards for obtaining pure filtered drinking-water for the sick.

15. Drainage and Sewerage.

No drain should ever pass under a hospital; all sinks, water-closets, lavatories, and baths, should be so placed that the drainage should be conveyed directly away, without passing under any part of the hospital. And for this purpose all drain pipes from them should be placed in the outer walls, but never against any inner wall of the building.

All drains or pipes for the purpose of conveying away water from any part of the hospital should be carefully trapped between the outer wall of the building and the sewer; and all drains should be ventilated. An excellent arrangement has been adopted at the Herbert Hospital, by which all the ward drainage is discharged into vertical drain pipes in the outer walls, which drain pipes are carried from a trap in the main drain below, straight up above the roof of the building, where they are left open to the air. This ensures thorough ventilation of the pipe, and prevents the possibility of the regurgitation of foul air into the building. A perforated box of charcoal is placed over the upper opening of the drain pipe to destroy any noxious gas that might otherwise escape into the air above the building.

16. Kitchen.

The kitchen should be placed away from the wards. Its walls and ceiling should be of light-coloured cement, for plaster has a tendency to fall off, from the vapour and effluvia of the kitchen.

Hospital cooking apparatus should be capable of doing two sets of cooking:—1. All the ordinary "diets." 2. Casual diets and "extras" for emergencies. It has been said that a good cook can cook with anything; but cooking in a hospital is a very important part of the general administration, and requires to be done with the utmost regularity, efficiency, and economy. In providing apparatus, it is necessary to consider how many "diets" of the same kind will be required; also what the nature of the cooking should be. Usually this consists of soups, farinaceous preparations, including puddings, stewed vegetables, roast joints, baked meat, or meat roasted in a roasting oven, broiled beef-steak or mutton-chop (there should be no frying in a hospital, except for fish, and even fish, cooked after the French plan, in oil, is better; if a patient can digest a fried steak, it is the best proof that he is fit to be discharged from hospital), tea and coffee. The "extra" articles usually required are beef-tea or warmed beef-juice, sago, &c. There should always be plenty of boiling water.

The dimensions, as well as the number of parts of which any hospital cooking apparatus should consist, will depend, of course, on the size of the hospital. The cheapest fuel for boiling liquids on a large scale is common coal. Where stewing has to be done on a large scale, steam is the best agent. For stewing on a small scale, and preparing extra articles at irregular times, gas is by far the most convenient fuel. But its use requires to be carefully restricted to such purposes, otherwise it will be found too costly. Roasting is now very well and economically done in ovens constructed for the purpose, with ordinary fuel. Gas ovens are sometimes convenient; but they are more expensive. Lately, many improved forms of hospital cooking apparatus, capable of performing these various processes, have been introduced. For small hospitals all the parts are generally combined in one small apparatus, placed in an ordinary kitchen fire-place. For large hospitals, the different parts are better separated. Of course, the same cooking apparatus and kitchen which answer for the patients are sufficient also for officers, nurses, and servants, although tea and breakfast will probably be made in the respective quarters of each.

The cooking apparatus, boilers, ovens, &c., if placed in the centre of the kitchen, after the French plan, instead of against the walls, will afford twice the amount of fire space.

17. WASH-HOUSE.

How to dispose of the Foul Linen.—Of course it should never be treasured up in any ward, scullery, or closet in the hospital. The sooner it is sent away and in the wash-tub the better. In hospitals of a few beds it should be thrown into a basket and carried straight away immediately; but in large hospitals, where changes are constantly going on, it is necessary to have ready means of conveying it out of the building, and for this purpose nothing answers so well as foul-linen shoots. These should be built in the wall. The best material for them is glazed earthenware piping, 15 to 18 inches in diameter. They should have an open mouth, also of earthenware; with a door, opening not near a ward, but from a staircase or well-ventilated passage. And they should end below in a small closet, out of which the linen should be taken as soon as the change is completed, and removed at once to the wash-house. To be quite safe, the pipe should be carried up to the roof of the building, though of a smaller diameter, to secure that the shaft is well ventilated.

Hospital washing should never be done in or close to a hospital. In a small hospital, the kitchen may be put in the basement, provided it is not under a ward, and it is very well ventilated; but the wash-house *never*. It at least should be always detached, and if within the hospital grounds at all, at the farthest attainable point in them, and to leeward. The reason, of course, is, that pure air in a hospital is the *sine quâ non*, while the surest method of obtaining foul air is to combine the excretions of the patients with the steam of hot water, and give access for this combined result to the sick by staircases or open windows.

The excellent new washing, drying, and wringing

machines lately invented are so numerous that it would take too long to enumerate them. On the whole, the laundry at the Wellington Barracks, which also washes for all the Guards' hospitals and barracks, and the new laundry at Haslar Naval Hospital, are the best I have seen. But every day brings in fresh inventions, and a reformer is always adopting the good ones. Admirable ones are attached to the new Herbert Hospital at Woolwich, and to Netley Hospital. The former is intended to wash for all the troops in garrison, as well as for the sick. I do not think that any reliable comparison has yet been made between the French system adopted at the Salpêtrière and Lariboisière hospitals and the English system. The French consists in filtering hot ley through the clothes, which are placed for that purpose in large tubs, with a compartment at the bottom, from which the ley is pumped up by machinery, and allowed to flow over the top of the linen, through which it filters into the compartment, to be again raised by the machine.

This plan is stated to be the most economical which has been tried in Paris.

The essential characteristic of the Haslar one is boiling by steam, the linen being afterwards placed in a rotating washing machine.

The method in use in the Wellington Barracks consists in passing the linen through slowly rotating washing tubs, in which it undergoes a process of *waulking* by wooden rods. This latter plan is both economical and effectual.

To ascertain which is the most really economical of the French and English plans, it would be necessary to inquire not only into the relative cost of washing, but into the relative wear and tear. The hardness or softness of the water must also be taken into account. The softer water is the cheaper, both in the consumption of soap and the wear and tear. Now the Paris water is in hardness to that of London as 20 to 16, and as 20 to 2 to that of Glasgow. Probably the Paris method is the only economical one with the Paris water. All the water used at the new Herbert Hospital, including that for the laundry, has a hardness of 13°, which will be reduced to $5\frac{1}{2}°$ by Dr. Clarke's softening process. This will effect a large economy in soap and linen, in addition to the advantage of having softer water for general hospital use.

Clean Linen Room.—After passing through the laundry, the linen is returned to the hospital for use; and any one who wishes to see perfect arrangements for storing and issuing clean linen must go to the Paris hospitals. Each hospital there is provided with one or more large well-lighted rooms, containing every arrangement for the mending, classification, and issuing of ward linen. The linen is *stacked* in open framework so as to admit currents of air through the piles—a thing of great importance.

This is a point of administrative detail in which all English hospitals are wofully behindhand. Even in the most recent plans I have seen, there has either been no provision of the kind, or it has been a mere half-dark closet. The mending room ought to be a separate room from the clean linen store, and adjoining. There should be besides in each ward a lock-up movable press, best placed under the sill of the large end window, with a table-leaf on hinges for folding, for such articles as may be stored in the ward.

18. Operating Theatres.

I need not say that surgical cases should never be placed higher than the first floor. It is important that an operating theatre should not only be on a level, but central between the men's and women's surgical wards. An operating theatre in a third story is very objectionable, particularly if patients have to be carried up a narrow flight of stairs and back after the operation has been performed. The proper place for an operating theatre is to be built out at the back of the centre; and the board-room may be under it. It is not uncommon, in small country hospitals, to have a recess or small room leading from the operating theatre, in which the patients remain until they have recovered, or at least recovered the immediate effects of the operation. But it is more and more becoming the practice of the best London hospitals to carry such patients back to their own ward, where it is believed (a belief in which I entirely concur) they have, if the ward is what it should be, better advantages, better chances, better care, nursing, and supervision. Of course there are exceptional cases, as in ovariotomy, trephining, &c., which may require to be by themselves. But this is for the surgeon to decide upon.

Operating theatres are best lighted by a good large skylight and a steady northern light from one large window, quite up to the ceiling. There must be no conflicting lights from different windows, and no southern aspect. Now, as the operating theatre is the only room in the hospital which ought to have one sole north light, this is very convenient, because it may occupy a situation which would not do for a ward.

We will next consider the application of these principles to the improvement of hospital plans.

IV.

IMPROVED HOSPITAL PLANS.

WITHIN the last few years very considerable advances have been made in hospital architecture in this country. A number of hospitals have been improved and added to on correct principles. Several new hospitals embodying these principles have been built, and the plans of many more are at present under discussion. The subject has also awakened renewed attention abroad; and quite recently two works of great importance have appeared on the subject in Paris. One of these is the "Etude sur les Hôpitaux," by M. Armand Husson, Director of the General Administration of the *Assistance Publique*, the other the "Rapport sur les Hôpitaux Civils de la Ville de Londres," by MM. Blondel and Ser, of the same bureau. These works afford information of great interest on the whole question of Hospital administration, and I am indebted to them for several illustrations introduced into these pages. I have had the opportunity also of examining a number of new hospital plans for buildings which it is proposed to construct in different parts of the country. They have all borne marks of careful study of the subject; but there are one or two points in which all of them present certain defects in common. I shall merely allude to these as points of experience, before proceeding to the general subject of this section.

One of the most common mistakes in hospital plans, even in some of the most recent of those I have seen, is mixing up together, in the same block, sick wards and administrative offices of all kinds. It need hardly be pointed out that such an attempt must necessarily lead to a very complicated structure, containing large wards and an indefinite number of rooms of different sizes, all connected by passages and stairs more or less dark, badly ventilated, and diffusing a common atmosphere throughout the building. By this arrangement of parts, all the old complications of badly constructed hospitals are reproduced in another form. The usual excuse is that it is cheaper than to separate the sick from the administration, which is extremely doubtful. One thing is not at all doubtful, that such an arrangement exposes both sick and administrators to very unnecessary risks, and is one of the causes of fever among the latter, already mentioned, a danger which should never be incurred on any plea of economy.

It is possible, no doubt, to ventilate more or less effectually a complicated building of this sort; but practically it will never be done.

Wherever any form of hospital construction requires much thought to be applied to its ventilation and other sanitary arrangements, it may be considered quite certain that the hospital is not a safe one for sick. Practically it is impossible to escape from this; viz., that safe hospital construction must, at whatever (apparent) cost, contain a maximum of facility and a minimum of difficulty for keeping every part of the building healthy.

It is a fundamental principle that the pavilions, whether single or double, should contain nothing but the sick and the offices immediately required for the ward. Everything else, board-rooms, chapels, quarters for officers and servants, except for the head nurse or nurses of each ward, stores, kitchens, laundries, should be placed in a separate building or buildings. It would be better even that convalescent rooms, where it is determined that there should be such rooms, should be out of the main building, but accessible under cover; for the obvious reason that convalescents require change of air which cannot be obtained under any circumstances in a hospital. The matron should always have her rooms as near to the nursing staff as possible. And as it is highly desirable that the day and night nurses of each ward should be kept as a separate staff, lodged as near to the head nurse as possible, if room can be found for these near their own pavilion, it is better.

Simplicity of construction, involving, as it should always do, a provision of abundant light and ventilation through every part of the hospital in which sick are placed, can only be secured in hospitals of any size by separating the administrative part from the sick part. The smallest country hospital should consist of at least two blocks of building.

The utmost simplicity of plan is an essential of good hospital construction. Complication of plan interferes with light, ventilation, discipline, facility of supervision. Every hole and corner, every passage, every small ward, which need not have been there, interferes with these four vital conditions of a good hospital. Every skulking place which can be spared must be avoided. As an invariable hospital rule, rather more than elsewhere in military hospitals, publicity may be considered as the best police and the best protection. It is far better that 30 patients should see the nurse's door than one or none. It is quite necessary that the chief ward attendant should be able to see the whole of her or his patients at once.

When the architect has arrived at a clear idea of what a hospital pavilion means—what it should contain and what it should not contain—the next important matter is to determine how the pavilions are to be arranged so as to form a

Plan No. III.

BUCKS INFIRMARY.

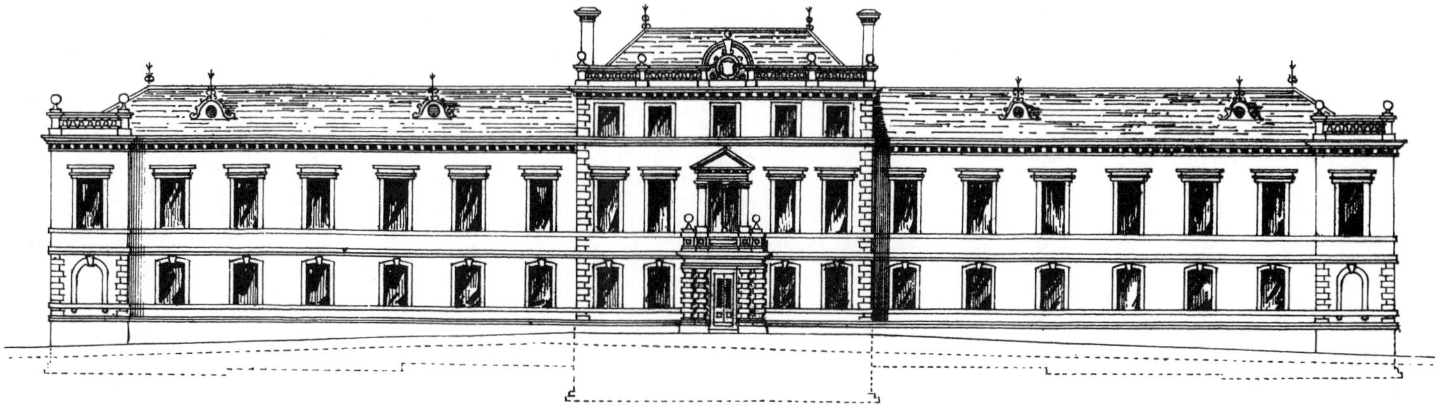

SOUTH ELEVATION.

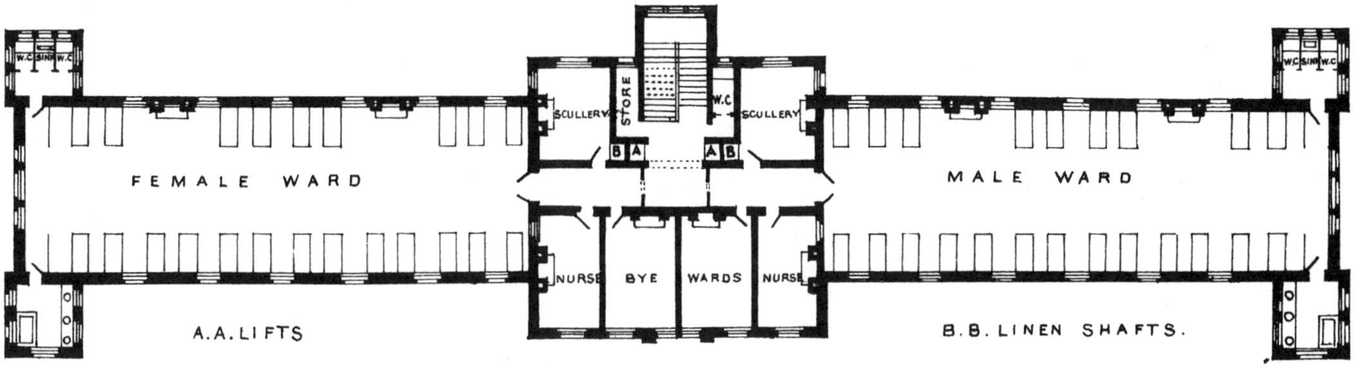

FIRST FLOOR PLAN

F. G. Netherclift, lith: 17 Mill Street, Conduit St. W.

London. Longman, Green & Co

hospital. From what has been said, it will be obvious that the arrangement of parts will depend on the number of beds for which the hospital is to be built. The following principles will enable a good block plan to be made.

1. Small Hospitals.

For hospitals intended to consist of two pavilions in line, the arrangement shown in fig. 16 might be followed. It consists of two wings, containing one ward on each floor of the wing, and a centre block for the administration.

Fig. 16.

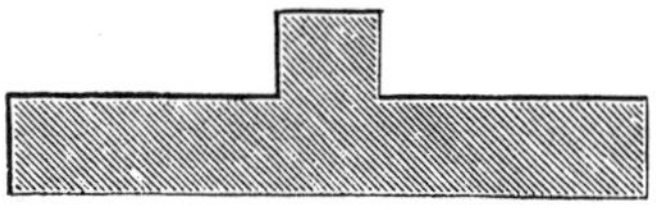

Two Pavilions in line.

A block plan of this kind, if erected in an airy position, would possess every requisite for health. The size of the administrative part of the building will depend upon the nature of the hospital management, and upon whether or not out-patients are to be received within the hospital.

When the administration is of very limited extent, the arrangement in fig. 16 would be unobjectionable. But as a general rule, and especially where out-patients have to be received, as much of the administrative part of the building as possible should be detached behind the main line of the hospital, in the manner shown in the regimental hospital plans, figs. 20, 21.

The plan and elevation of the New Bucks Infirmary (No. 3), intended for 52 beds, with the offices on the ground floor, and wards 16 feet high on the first floor, built by

Mr. Brandon, is the most recently completed civil hospital on the new plan, and has been found to answer very well.

When the number of beds for which the hospital is intended exceeds what can be accommodated in a double pavilion of this form, the plan shown in fig. 17 may be adopted. This fig. shows a building consisting of two double pavilions and a centre. Wherever this form is adopted, the pavilions should be entirely cut off from the centre by spacious staircases carried up where the centre joins the pavilions. In a hospital of this form the centre should be one floor in height; the pavilions would be in two floors.

FIG. 17.

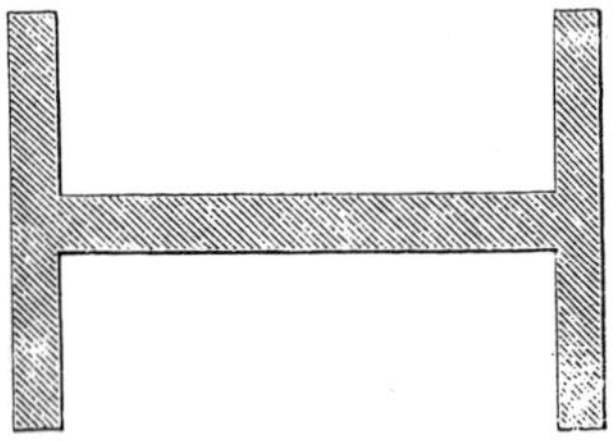

Hospital of two double Pavilions and Centre.

A similar arrangement of parts is shown in fig. 18. In this case the administration is a separate block, two or three floors in height, connected with the pavilions, two floors in height, by a centre one floor in height.

FIG. 18.

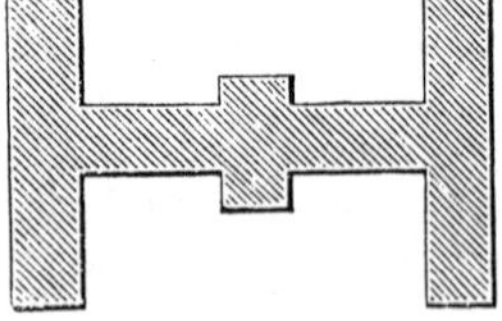

Hospital of double Pavilion Wings with central administration.

Fig. 19 is one half of fig. 17, and consists of three pavilions, radiating from a common centre. If this plan is adopted, there should be a large central staircase at the point of junction.

FIG. 19.

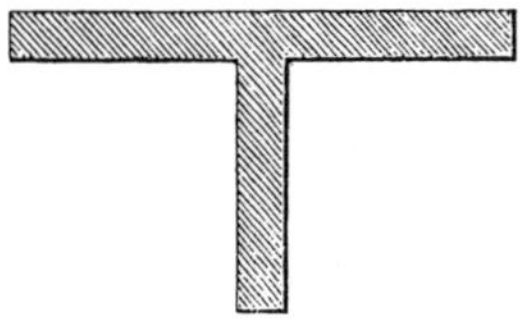

Double Pavilion Hospital with projecting Centre.

Another application of the pavilion principle is shown in figs. 20 and 21, and is adapted for regimental hospitals, either for cavalry or infantry. For a full cavalry regiment one floor is sufficient. For an infantry regiment, double the accommodation is required; and the building is then erected in two floors. This is simply one of the double pavilions of the Herbert Hospital, with so much of the administration as is absolutely necessary arranged between the wards; the remainder being in a block behind.

Several cavalry hospitals on this plan have been constructed, and they are found to answer admirably.

A pavilion hospital on the same plan is proposed for Malta, to receive the sick from barracks on the Cotonera side of the great harbour.

These examples of block plans are taken from existing hospitals. The object, in buildings of this class, is to bring all parts of the hospital under one roof, more with a view to facility of communication throughout, than to securing the sanitary state of the hospital. Such plans can only be used within certain limits. As a rule it is safer to consider every pavilion, containing the largest number of sick a pavilion ought

FIG. 20.

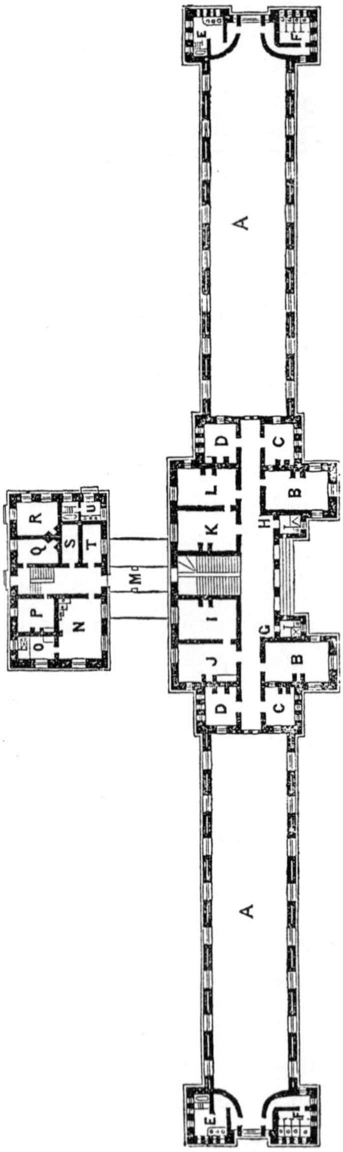

Ground Plan of a Regimental Hospital for 120 Beds.

A B. Wards.
C. Nurses' Rooms.
D. Sculleries.
E. Baths and Lavatories.
F. Sinks.

G H. Small-Ward Offices.
I. Orderlies.
J. Hospital Serjeant.
K. Day-Room and Waiting-Room.
L. Surgery.
M to U. Kitchen, Stores, &c.

FIG. 21.

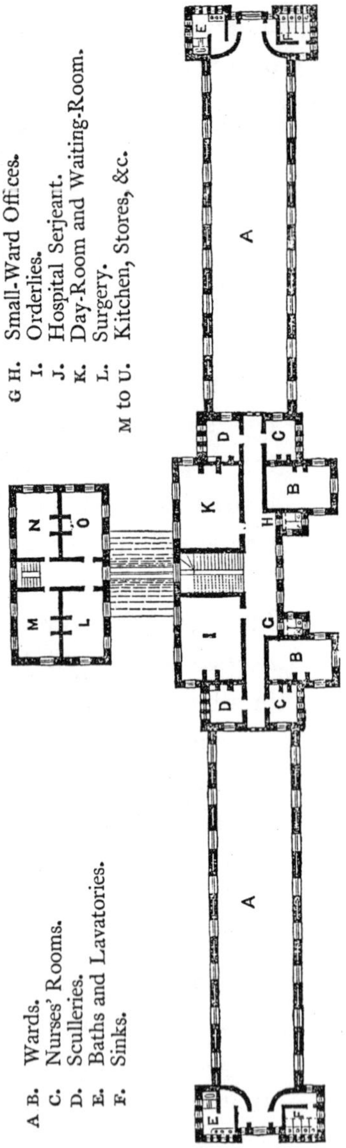

First Floor Plan.

to contain, as a separate hospital, and to connect all the pavilions together in such a way as to insure a separate ventilation for each block.

2. Large Hospitals.

I next ask, what should be the arrangement of parts in the larger class of hospitals?

Fortunately we have a number of examples in different parts of Europe of excellent arrangement of parts in block plans. No doubt all the older hospitals of this class admit of considerable improvements in detail. But the block plan can be studied by itself with great advantage. I shall choose a few examples illustrative of existing hospitals—of hospitals in the progress of construction and of plans completed but not yet carried into execution.

Fig. 22 is the block plan of St. Bartholomew's Hospital,

Fig. 22.

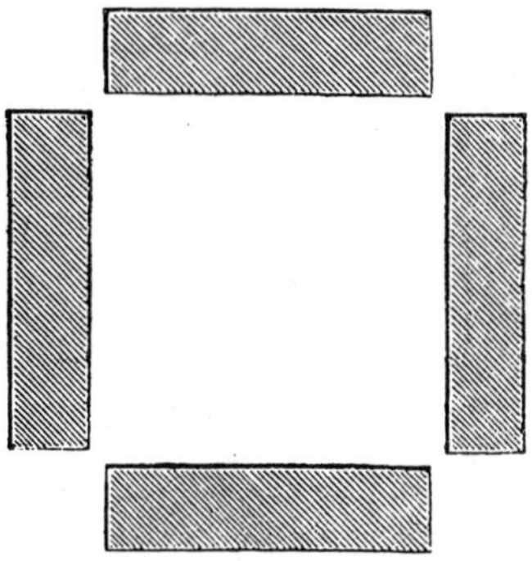

Block Plan of St. Bartholomew's Hospital.

showing four pavilions arranged at right angles to each other, with the corners open to admit of the circulation of air. In such a hospital each block might be a double pavilion, each in two floors, and each pavilion might contain two wards with their offices on each floor. The advantages of this plan are compactness of structure, and a corresponding facility in administration, together with open angles to allow of circulation of air in the court. The disadvantages are that the means of communication must either be in the open air in all weathers, or under a verandah or corridor carried along one side of the lower floor wards, partially obstructing the light and ventilation. All the sides of the hospital could not be thoroughly exposed to the sun's rays, summer and winter, although this ground of objection would be diminished by placing two of the open opposite angles north and south.

Fig. 23 is an illustration of the same block plan as it exists

FIG. 23.

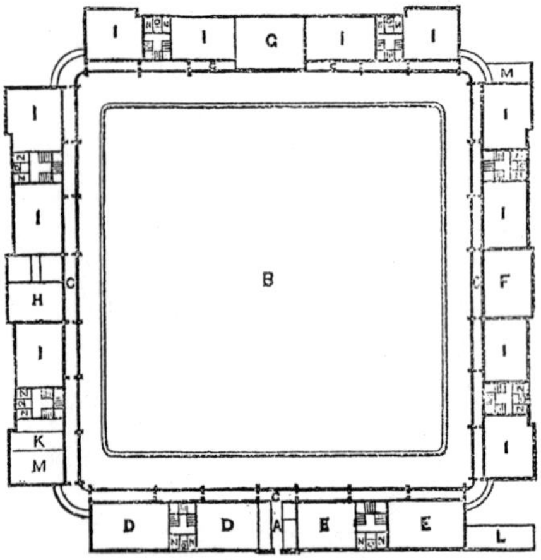

Ground Plan of Naval Hospital, Yarmouth.

A Entrance Archway.
B Garden.
C Open-arched Corridor, one story high, surrounding the garden.
D Rooms for sick officers.
E Steward's stores.
F Chapel.
G First Floor, Operating Theatre: Ground Floor, Billiard Room.
H Committee Room, Surgery, &c.
I I I Wards, 14 beds each.
K Padded Room.
L Bath Rooms, Wash-house, &c.
M M Sculleries.
N N Nurses' Rooms.
O O Water Closets.

at Yarmouth Naval Hospital. This is a very good building, one of the best, indeed, of the older hospitals in Great Britain. The pavilions are on two floors only, they are wide enough apart at the corners to admit the sea breeze into the court, and every part of the building is connected by an arched corridor along the ground floor. This corridor of course partially

FIG. 24.

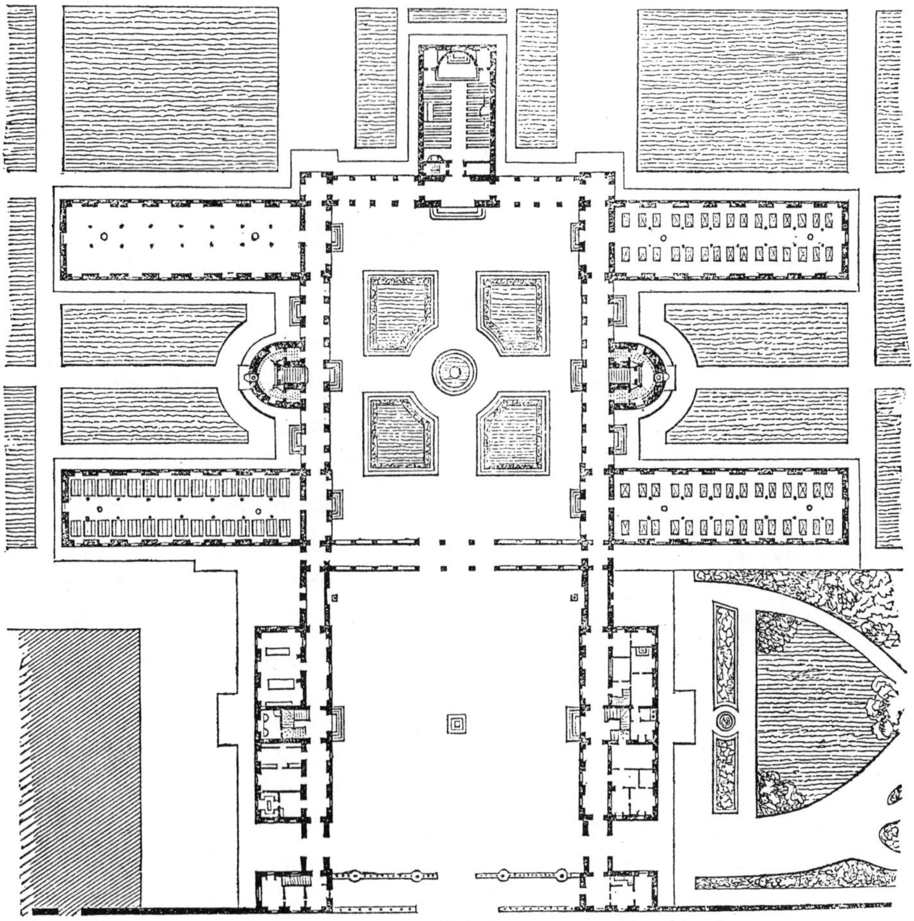

Fondation Brezin (Hospice de la Reconnaissance) at Garches.

obstructs the light of the wards. The ward details, as shown in the plan, are not altogether in accordance with modern requirements; but they could easily be made so in any future applications of the same principle. And the lower floor wards should be raised on basements to such a height as to admit of the connecting corridor being carried round the building below the level of the ward windows.

An exceedingly simple arrangement of pavilions is shown in fig. 24, which gives a ground plan of the "Fondation Brezin," at Garches. All the administrative parts of the building are in separate blocks. The pavilions and chapel are also separate, and all are connected by a simple corridor carried past the end of the blocks.

I do not propose this as a *hospital* plan. It will be seen at once that it is deficient in proper hospital details. But it contains the pavilion arrangement reduced to its utmost simplicity for purposes of health and facility of administration. (This building is in fact planned for infirm, and not for sick.) It contains the germ of the hospital construction adopted for Lariboisière, of which here is a plan (No. 4).

The famous Lariboisière Hospital consists of six detached single pavilions for sick, two pavilions in the front for administration, two behind for the sisters and nurses and for the washing establishment, with chapel, operation-rooms, baths, &c., in detached buildings, at the end furthest from the entrance. Between the pavilions is a range of one-story rooms, used for dining-rooms, &c. The pavilions contain 3 floors of wards, one large ward for 32 beds, and one small ward for two beds at the far end of it, on each floor. Each floor has a sister's room and scullery; and a spacious staircase gives access to the wards. All the pavilions are connected by an arched glazed corridor, one floor in height, over which is an open terrace, used by con-

PARIS
HOPITAL DE LARIBOISIÈRE.
612 BEDS.

A. Offices

B. Kitchen On the Ground Floor. On the 1st Floor Lodgings of the Officers On the 2nd Floor Dormitories for Male Attendants

C. On the Ground Floor Pharmacy. On the First Floor Lodgings of the Officers, On the 2nd Floor, Rooms of the Resident Pupils.

D.E.F.G.H.I.J.K. Dining Rooms &c, One Story high.

L.M.N.O.P.Q. Buildings for the Sick. Three Stories high.

R. Ground Floor Washhouse. On the 1st Floor Linen Store. 2nd Floor Dormitories for Female Attendants

S. Sister's Rooms. T. U. Baths. V Chapel

XY Amphitheatre

Z. Manege & Stores

W. Stable and Dead House

a.a.a.a. Corridor one story high, with open Terrace above, running round the buildings, and connecting them

b.b.b. Gardens

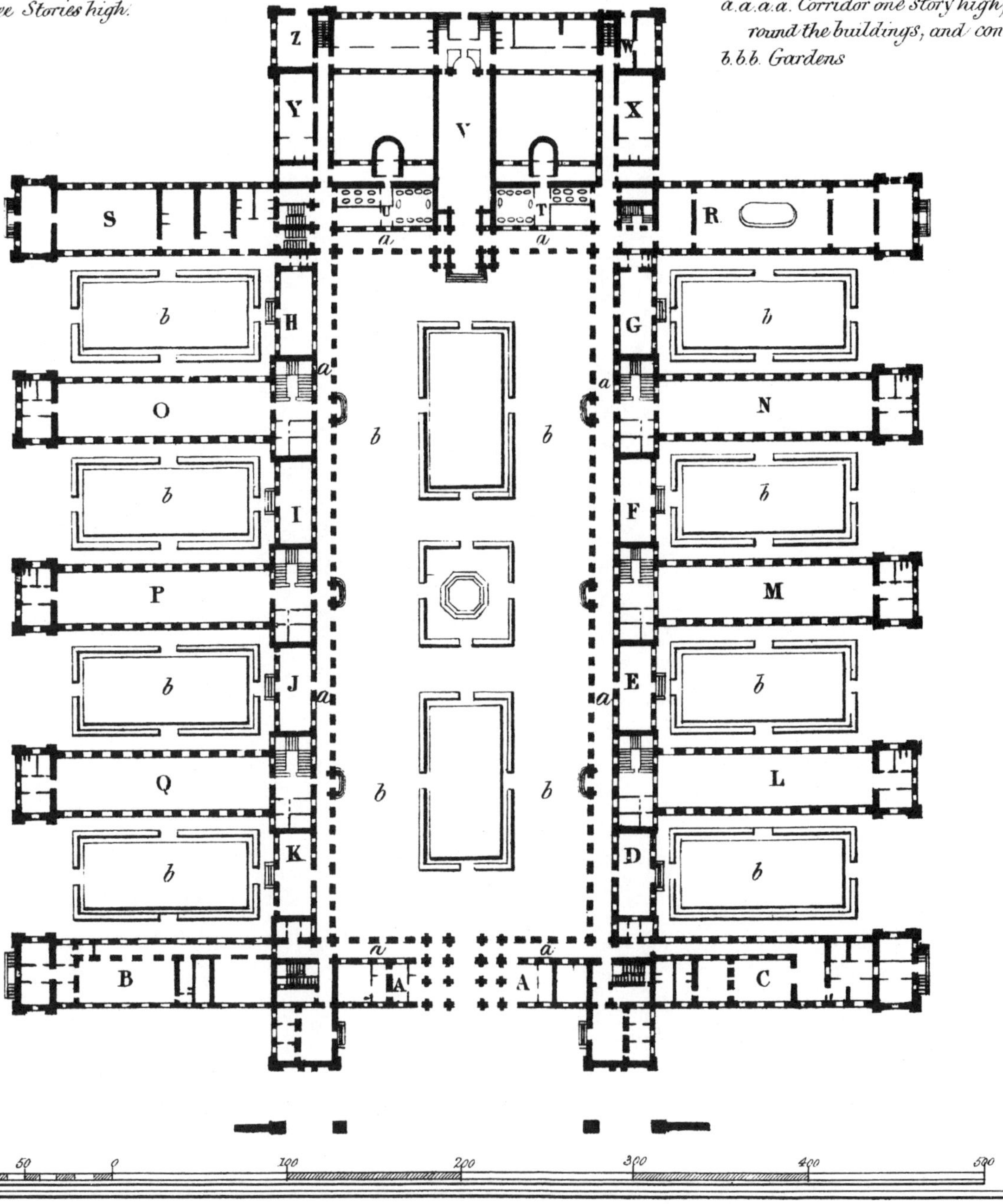

F. G. Netherclift, Lith. 1st Mill Street, Conduit St.

London Longman Green & Co.

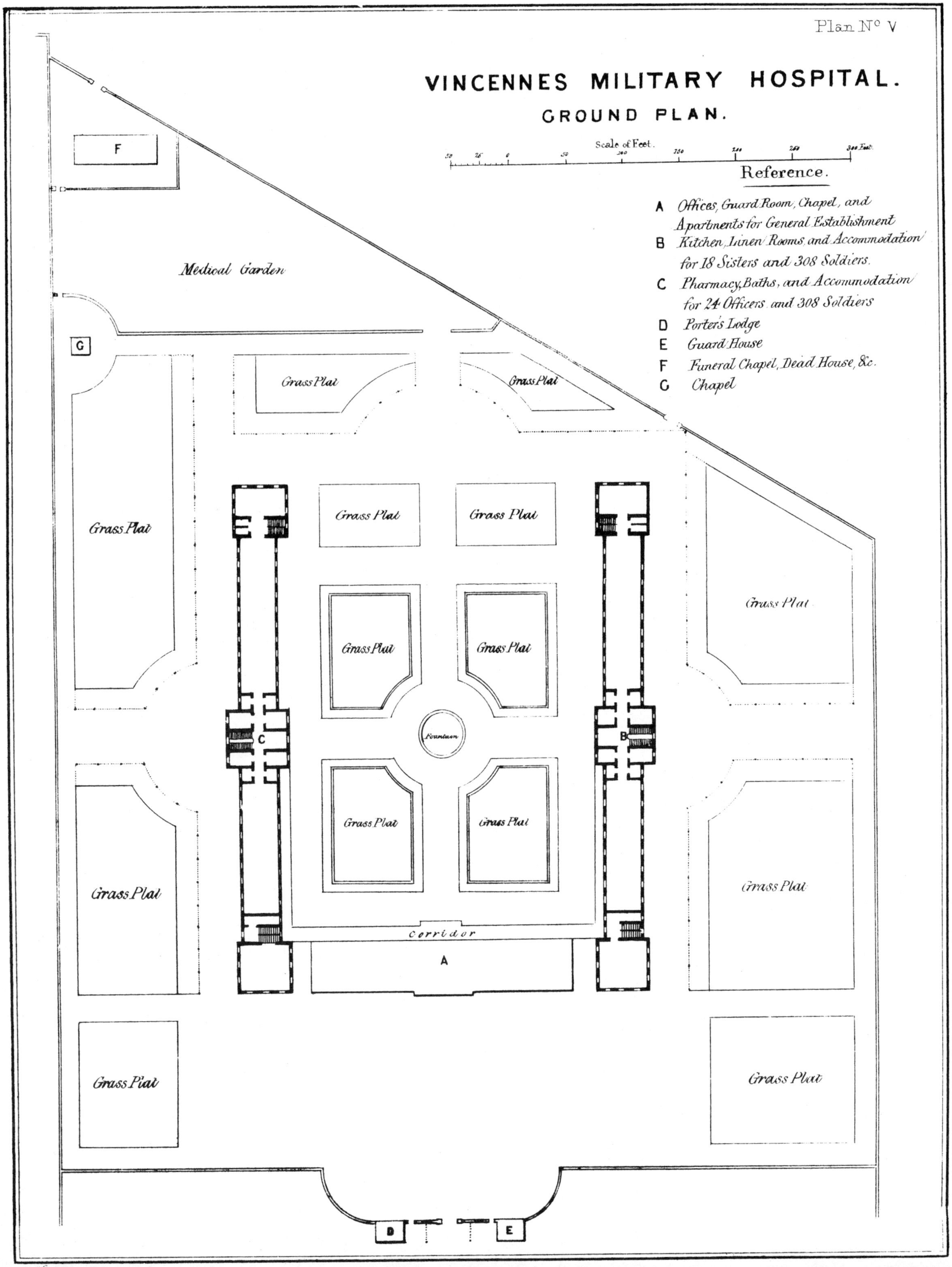
Plan No. V
VINCENNES MILITARY HOSPITAL.
GROUND PLAN.
Scale of Feet.
50 25 0 50 100 150 200 250 300 Feet.
Reference.
A Offices, Guard Room, Chapel, and Apartments for General Establishment
B Kitchen, Linen Rooms, and Accommodation for 18 Sisters and 308 Soldiers.
C Pharmacy, Baths, and Accommodation for 24 Officers and 308 Soldiers
D Porter's Lodge
E Guard House
F Funeral Chapel, Dead House, &c.
G Chapel
Medical Garden
Grass Plat
Fountain
Corridor
A
B
C
D
E
F
G

F. G. Netherclift lith. 17 Mill Street, Conduit St.

valescents, and also as a means of access between the first floors, when the weather permits. The hospital contains 612 beds, divided amongst six separate pavilions, which are just as much distinct hospitals as if they were miles from each other. The block plan of this hospital is excellent, but the pavilions are too close together for their height; or, rather, there should have been only two floors of wards instead of three. The small wards are badly placed, away from the sister, and close to the *open privies* of the ward. This hospital is warmed and ventilated, unfortunately, by artificial means, and has presented the anomaly, easily resolved by those acquainted with the sanitary requirements for sick, of one of the best hospitals in existence, so far as the block plan is concerned, yielding one of the highest rates of mortality.

There is another hospital, the St. Jean, at Brussels, built upon a similar plan; and also a hospital at Bordeaux.

The Vincennes Military Hospital, for 637 beds, of which I give a ground plan (No. 5), shows another arrangement of pavilions. In this example, the pavilions for sick are double, with wards for non-commissioned officers, and rooms for sisters at the two extreme ends, but cut off by separate staircases. These pavilions form two sides of a square, the third side is formed by a block containing the chapel and the administrative offices and quarters. The fourth side of the square is open to the country. Each pavilion consists of three floors and an attic, and is connected with the administration by a glazed corridor as far as the central staircases. It consists, in fact, of two hospitals, one for 308, the other for 332 sick, connected with one administration common to both. The disadvantages of the plan are that, if the whole building were used, there would be three floors and an attic occupied by sick, instead of two floors only. The ward details are also objectionable in some important points.

One advantage of the double pavilion adopted in this plan must be mentioned; and that is, the facility with which a large number of sick can be superintended and nursed on the same floor, instead of entailing on the attendants the amount of running up and down stairs required in the Lariboisière plan. The Vincennes wards, however, are built for rather too many beds. But, on the other hand, the building is in an open, elevated situation in the country; and each pavilion is divided from top to bottom by an unusually spacious staircase up to the roof. It is ventilated and warmed by the draught of a chimney and hot-water vessels.

All the advantages of the Vincennes and Lariboisière plans, without any of their disadvantages, and with greatly improved sanitary arrangements, will be realized in the new Herbert Hospital now under construction at Woolwich. (Plan No. 6.)

This, when completed, will be by far the finest hospital establishment in the united kingdom, or indeed in Europe. It consists of four double and three single pavilions, with the ends in the free air. All the wards are raised on basements, those at the lower end of the ground are so lofty as to afford excellent accommodation for the museum, library, medical officers' rooms, board-rooms, and stores. There are only two floors of wards to each pavilion, and the distance between the pavilions is double the height of the pavilion, measured from the floor of the lowest ward. Every ward has a large end window, commanding beautiful views; and the ablution and bath accommodation, together with water-closets, is placed in the free atmosphere at the end of the wards. Each large ward contains from 28 to 32 beds, with windows along the opposite

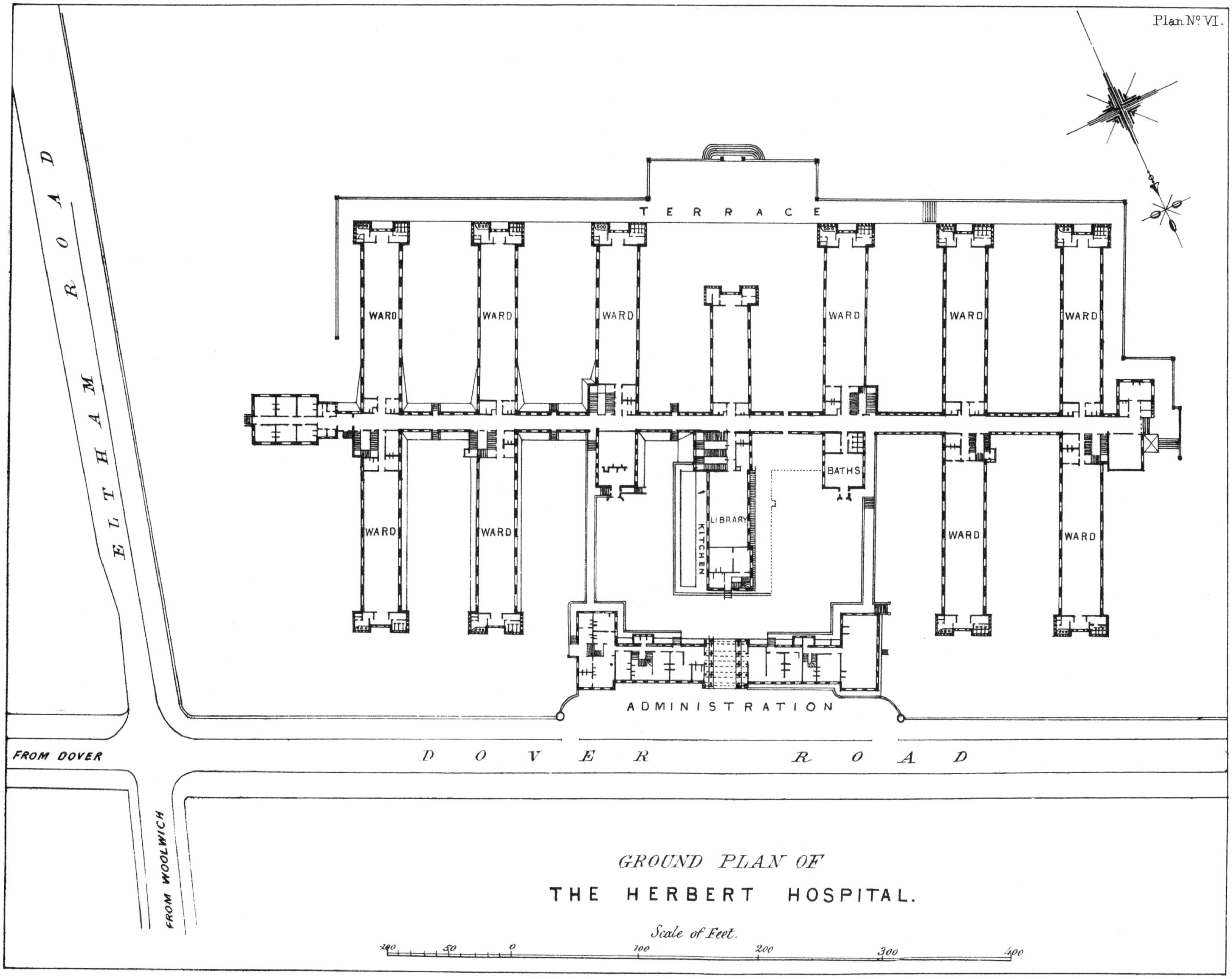

GROUND PLAN OF

THE HERBERT HOSPITAL.

London: Longman, Green & Co

sides, one for every two beds; and each ward has a nurse's room and scullery. Unfortunately the army regulation number of cubic feet per bed has limited the height of the wards to 14 feet. There is a convalescents' day-room in the central pavilion. The kitchen is in a basement, also in the centre; over it there is a library, and over the library the chapel. All the administrative offices and quarters are in a separate block in front. The axis of the wards is a little to the E. of north; and each side will receive the sun's rays during some part of the day. At one end of the hospital there are separate lunatic wards with separate offices. At the other end is the operation theatre, with a few small wards for special cases. The total accommodation is for 650 beds, in 7 detached buildings, all connected together through the centre by a corridor one floor in height, with a basement corridor beneath, through which the whole of the service of the hospital, so far as regards the conveyance of diets, medicines, coals, and the removal of dust and foul linen, will be carried out. This is effected by a system of lifts and shoots. And the result will be, that the usual bustle observed in hospital passages will be altogether avoided. This hospital embodies the great administrative principle of an entire separation between what is immediately necessary for the sick and what is not so, and yet without interfering with the efficiency of the administration. Over the corridor there is an open terrace, to which convalescents in the first-floor wards will have easy access in fine weather. And the covered corridor below will be available for exercise in wet weather. Each ward is 26½ feet wide and 14 feet high, and each bed has 93 to 97 superficial feet, and, 1200 to 1400 cubic feet. The walls will have a polished light-coloured surface. It is intended to warm the wards by two open fire-places along the centre of the wards, the flues being carried under the floor, and used for warming the air admitted to the wards. The floors are of iron beams, filled in with concrete, and covered with oak boarding. The whole will be fire-proof, and the sick in the lower wards will not suffer from noise in the wards overhead. Hot and cold water will be laid over the entire building; and the supply, which is taken from chalk, and hard, will be softened by the lime process before being transmitted to the hospital.

In Malta it is proposed to erect a general military hospital on the pavilion principle for 300 beds, with the pavilions differently arranged from any existing example. A ground plan of this proposed hospital is given in Plan No. 7. The site, chosen as the most healthy in the garrison, is limited, and the arrangement of parts has to be conformed to the shape of the ground. But so flexible is the pavilion construction that it suits itself readily to this requirement. There will be six pavilions arranged side by side, each containing two floors of wards, and the whole connected by open arcades sufficient to afford shelter for sun and rain, but to leave ventilation perfectly free. The entire administration is detached and placed in front of the hospital; but all parts of it are connected by convenient staircases with the corridors. The walls on the sides towards the sun, and the roof will be double to ensure coolness. The hospital will overlook the sea at a height of 170 feet above its level.

Other two establishments are proposed to be erected by the enlightened local government of Malta. One of these is an asylum for 1000 aged and infirm persons, 500 of each sex. A ground plan of this proposed establishment is given, Plan No. 8. It consists of eight pavilions, each two floors in height, arranged in two squares, containing in all 29 wards for beds, with dining-rooms on the ground-floor. To each square there is a day-room placed in the centre. The whole

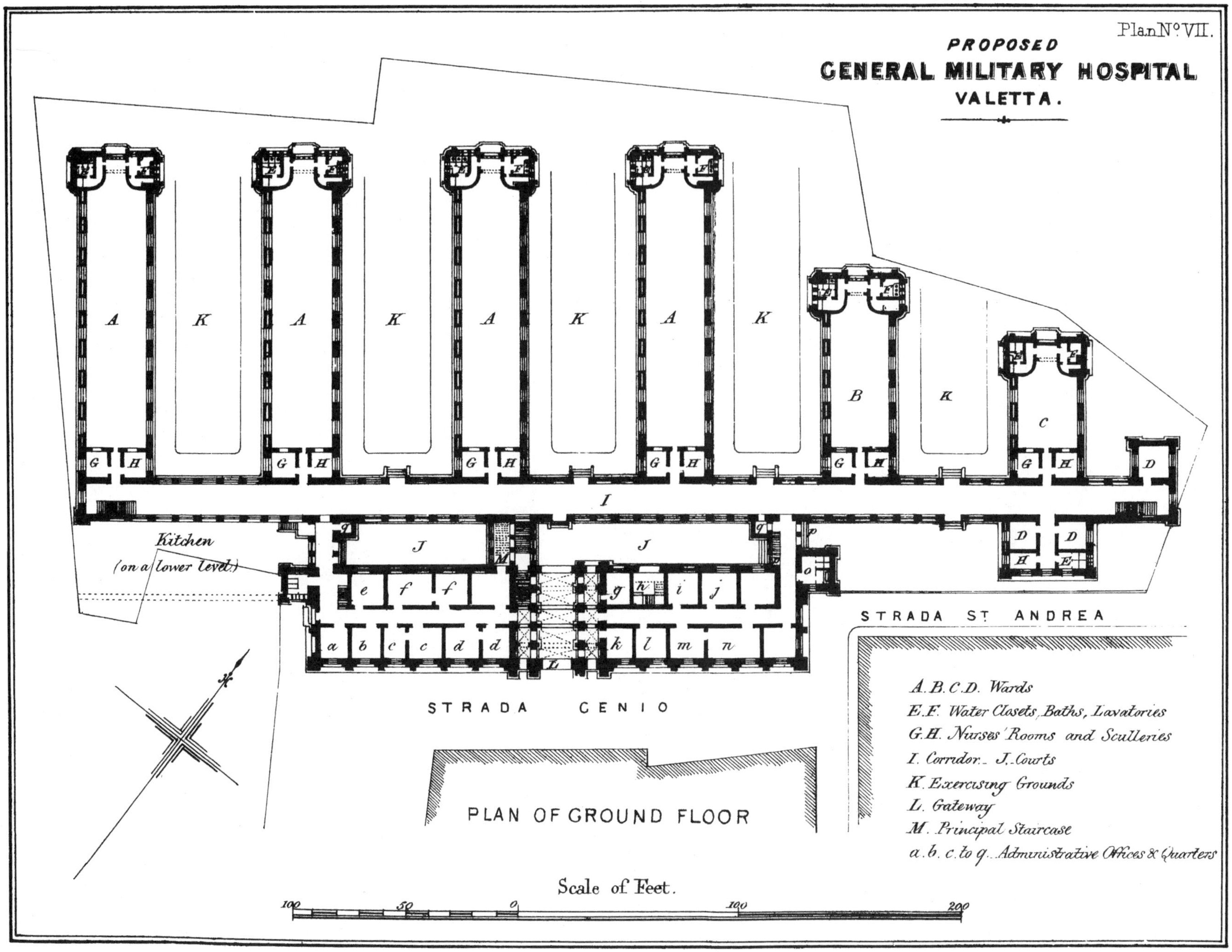

F. G. Netherclift, Lith: 17 Mill Street

London. Longman, Green & C°

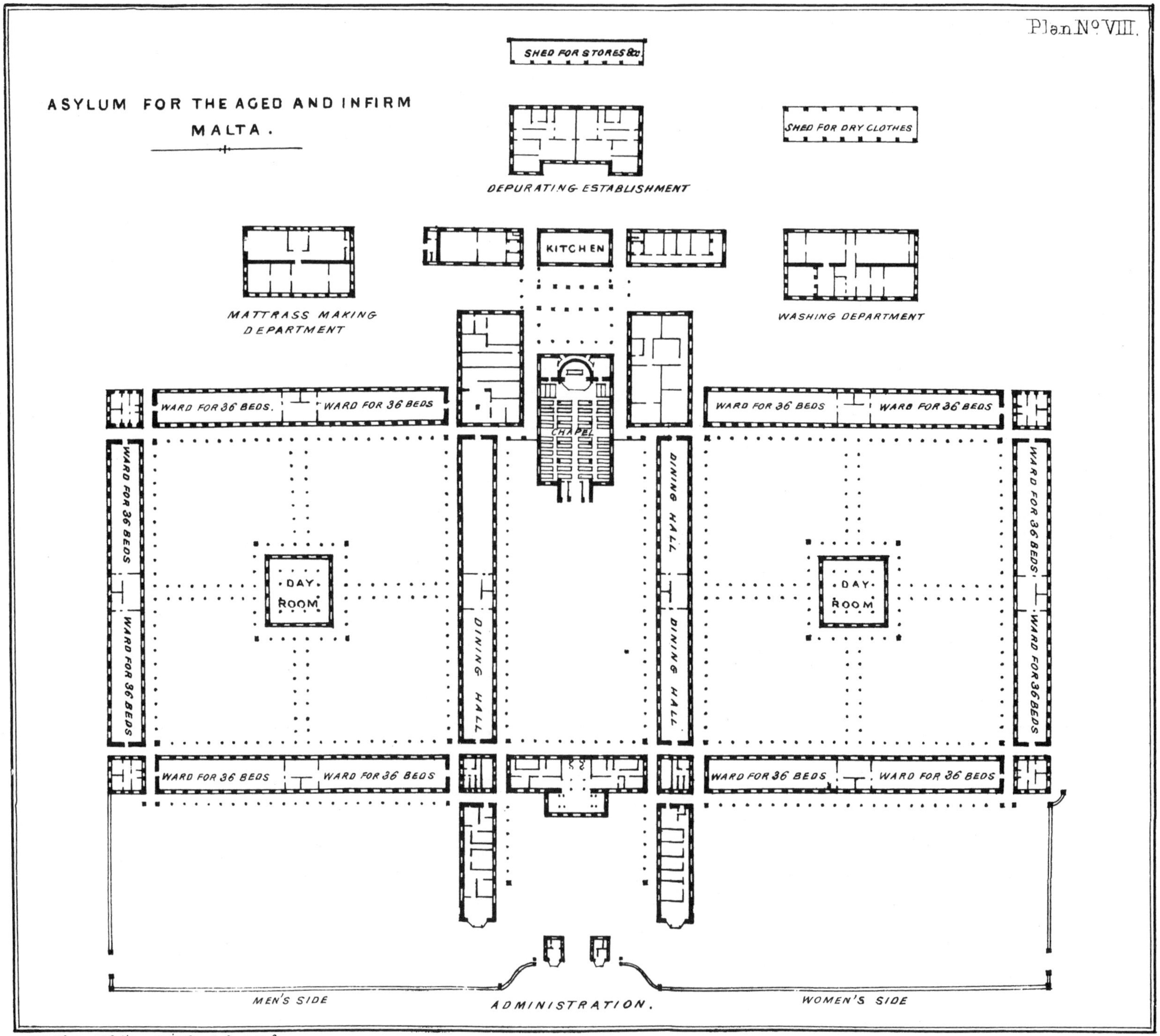

F. G. Netherclift Litho 27 Mill Street, Conduit St.

London Longman, Green & Cº

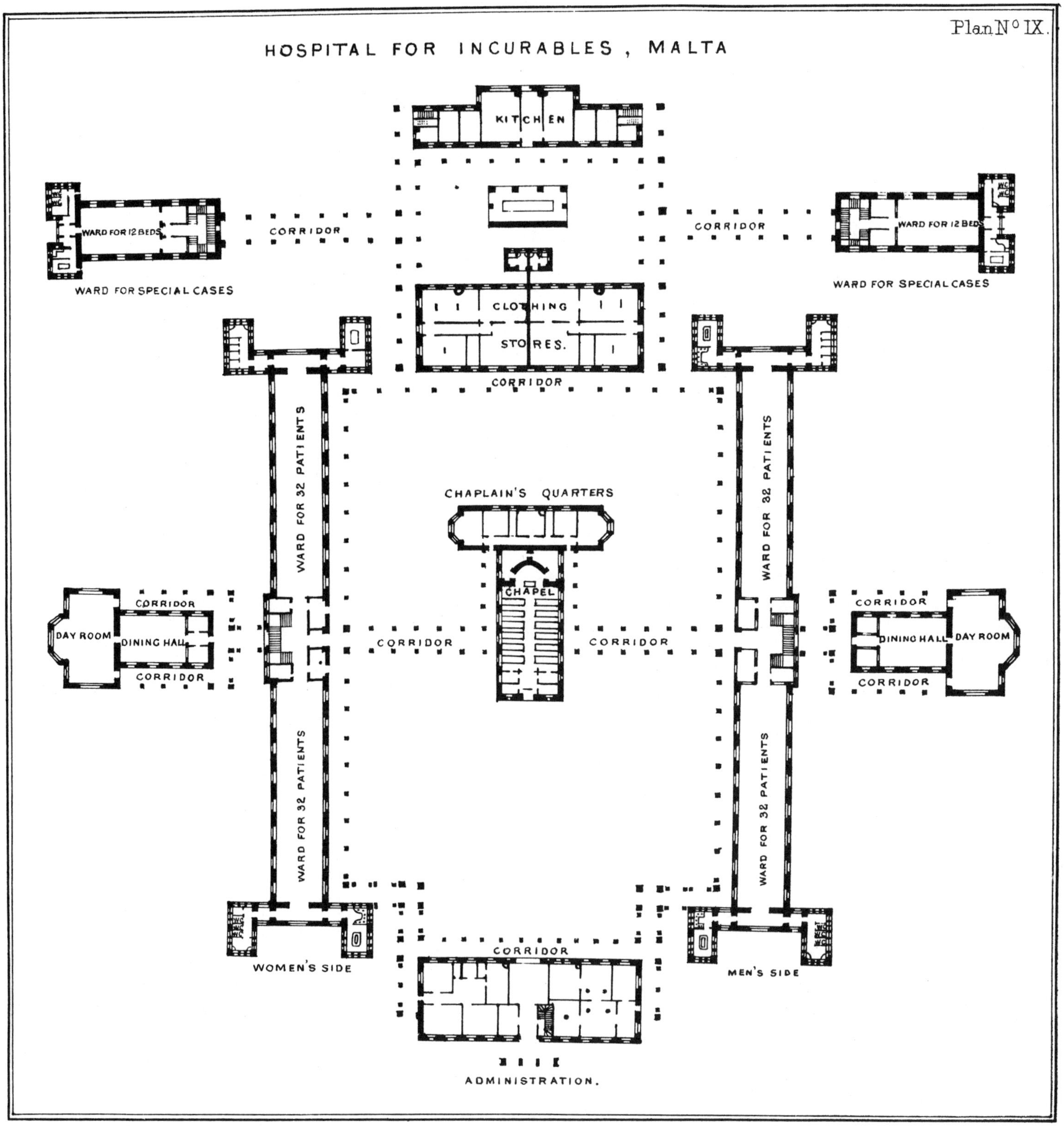

F. G. Netherclift, lith.: 17 Mill Street, Conduit St. W.

London. Longman, Green & Co.

establishment is connected by open arcades, with terraces over. Every block throughout the entire establishment is detached from every other. And the latrines, lavatories, and baths, which will be on the most improved English construction, are in detached square blocks in the angles, and accessible from the wards under open arcades. The administrative portion of the building is very complete, and the whole exemplifies an arrangement which, with some alterations in detail, might be adopted for a hospital of the same number of sick, if it ever were considered necessary to bring so many together.

Connected with this establishment, it is proposed to build a hospital for 300 beds, on a plan shown in No. 9. This consists of two long pavilions similar in construction to those of the Herbert Hospital, and two smaller detached blocks for the treatment of special or offensive cases. It will be observed that each of the larger blocks has a dining-room and day-room—a matter of necessity in this building, for a considerable proportion of its inmates will be incurable, not acute cases.

The sanitary details of both plans contain everything required for ensuring a healthy state of the buildings. They were prepared at the instance of the government of Malta, by Mr. T. H. Wyatt; and when completed, they will place this small island in the foremost rank as regards its charitable institutions.

These illustrations of hospital construction, when compared with what has been the past practice in this country, will show at once what ought to be done, and what ought not to be done, in planning buildings to be occupied by sick or maimed.

Some recent plans, however, have, alas! reproduced all the old errors in a novel form. Sometimes the wards have been improved in proportions, in light and facilities for ventilation, while the arrangements for baths, lavatories, and water-closets have been most objectionable. In other instances, kitchens and other offices have been placed under the sick wards, while the wards themselves were good. Again, as already mentioned, the administrative parts of the building have been so mixed up with the portions allotted for sick as to introduce all the old objectionable dark corners and useless passages which constitute so large a proportion of the worst class of hospital buildings. Mistakes such as these can only be avoided by a very careful study and application of the principles laid down. It should never be forgotten that the first thing to be considered is what is best for the sick, not what may appear to be cheapest—for the cheapness is only apparent—not what will make a good architectural elevation, for this is a point quite beside the question.

The very first condition to be sought in planning a building is, that it shall be fit for its purpose. And the first architectural law is, that fitness is the foundation of beauty. The hospital architect may feel assured that, only when he has planned a building which will afford the best chance of speedy recovery to sick and maimed people, will his architecture and the economy which he seeks, be realized.

V.

CONVALESCENT HOSPITALS.

It is a rule without any exception, that no patient ought ever to stay a day longer in hospital than is absolutely essential for medical or surgical treatment. What, then, is to be done with those who are not yet fit for work-a-day life? Every hospital should have its convalescent branch, and every county its convalescent home.

The first necessity of a convalescent hospital is that it should not be like a hospital at all: and the very best kind of convalescent hospital would be a string of cottages. The reason for this is fourfold:—

1. To get rid of the idea of being in hospital altogether from the minds of the inmates, and to substitute for it that of home. As long as they are hospital inmates, they feel as hospital inmates, they think as hospital inmates, they act as hospital inmates, not as people recovering.

2. To secure a more free and bracing atmosphere than can ever be secured in any building containing a large number of inmates.

3. Because cottages may be more slightly built, and therefore are less expensive than large, complicated, solid buildings.

4. Because in the point of view of moral discipline it is yet more important to separate men from women among convalescents than among the sick. And of course this can be done much more easily and efficiently, and with far less trouble

to the administration, in separate houses than in separate parts of the same house.

It is almost needless to repeat the A B C of all sanitary lessons—that the best building, intended to hold a large number of inmates, can never be made so healthy as a cottage for a small number, if well constructed.

All rules against curtains, against washing in the dormitory, &c., which *must* be maintained in hospitals, may be relaxed, at all events on the female side, in a properly built Convalescent Home. It should be a home. Each bed should be separated by a rod and iron staple, and curtain, about 6 or 7 feet high (to be pulled far back in the daytime) from the next bed; and a wash-hand-stand should be permitted within this compartment.

The number of beds for which each ward, whether for men or women, is constructed, should not exceed six, or be less than three: almost every hospital condition, in fact, is reversed.

The indispensable hospital rule, that no patient should be sent to or admitted into the kitchen or ward scullery, is also reversed in a convalescent home, where the more the patients are occupied, the better. The men who are able for it should be employed in the garden, which is better for them than their in-door trades. The women who are able for it should do nearly all the household work, at least on their own side; and a little sick cookery may well be taught them in the kitchen, but on a hot-plate, as convalescents should not be called upon to stand long at a hot kitchen fire.

That all this must be done with discretion, and in subordination to the necessity of giving the convalescents constant fresh air, and as much as possible of it out of doors, it is almost needless to say.

Some convalescents will want entire rest ; and this, with fresh air and good food, will be the main element of their recovery. This will be the case with those forms of uterine disease now sadly common among young female servants, from the use of stiff stays, and form of petticoats hanging from the waist. Others will be able to walk and yet not able to use their arms to do household work. With all, much care will be needed to prevent them damping their feet or clothes.

The medical officer and head sisters will have to exercise constant vigilance in this matter of occupation.

There are as yet few convalescent establishments. And as it is most probable that this class of accommodation will be extended, it is important to observe correct principles in future plans.

Here are two or three illustrations of different kinds of buildings.

Fig. 25 is a plan of the first floor of the Convalescent Institution at Walton-on-Thames. On the left are 4 women's wards, opening from a common inner passage. There is a corresponding number of men's wards on the right hand side of the plan. There is one ward for 9 beds, 2 wards for 11 beds each, one ward for 12, one for 13, two for 14 and one for 15. The projecting ward behind, called the Ellesmere Ward, is for 18 beds. The cubic feet per bed vary from 459 to 874, the average being about 628 cubic feet per bed. There are 117 beds on a floor, all of which, except 18 (in the Ellesmere Ward) are in rooms opening from inner passages, and having windows on one side only. The Ellesmere Ward has windows on three sides. In general construction the building can only be considered as an inferior model of a provincial hospital. It is a praiseworthy attempt to meet a great want;

but its details should certainly not be followed in future institutions.

FIG. 25.

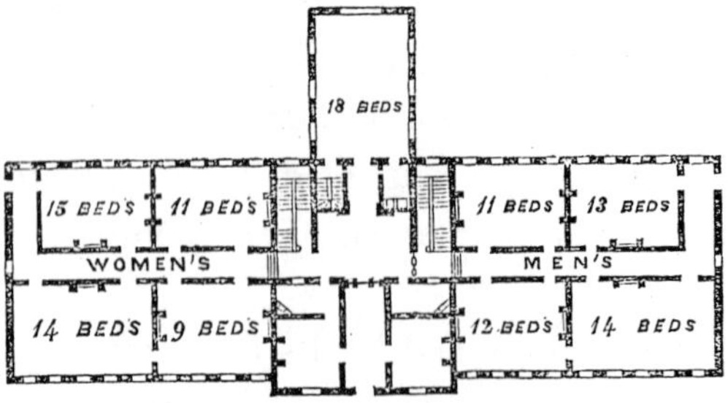

First Floor Plan of the Convalescent Institution, Walton-on-Thames.

Fig. 26 is a sketch plan of the Male Convalescent Institution founded by the Emperor at Vincennes. It is constructed on a totally different principle from the English one. It consists of a long series of three-bedded rooms, bent on itself at right angles, so as to form partial courts, the whole being connected by a corridor for communication. The arrangement of parts is simple and ingenious, while it enables a large number of rooms to obtain the benefit of direct light and air through the outer wall. For an interesting account of this establishment, *vide* Note, p. 116, and the following sketch plan (for it is only a sketch to show the general arrangement), I am indebted to Colonel Clark Kennedy, who was kind enough to go over the establishment for the purpose.

It will be seen at once wherein this building differs in design from the preceding. In the first place, it has no internal corridor. It has a corridor along one end of all the rooms; but the arch of the corridor, the door of the room, and the window at the opposite end of the room, are all in one line, so that a thorough ventilation is easily effected. Again, the rooms are intended each for three beds only—a

Fig. 26.

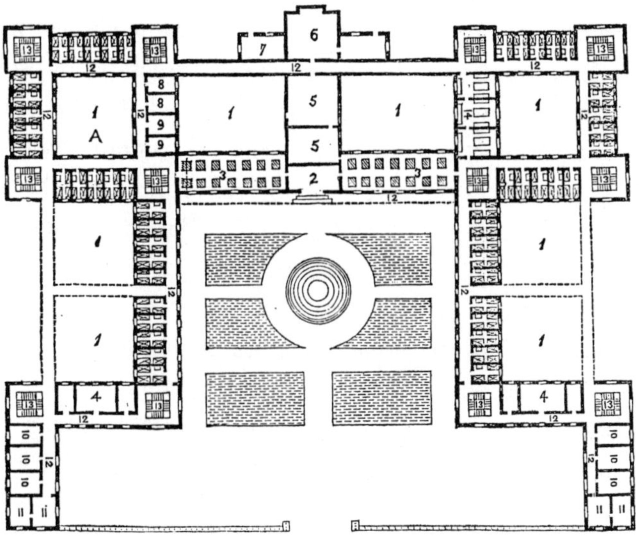

Sketch Plan of Male Convalescent Institution, Vincennes.

1 Courts.
2 Chapel.
3 Refectory.
4 Parlour.
5 Kitchen.
6 Laundry.
7 Baths.
8 Pharmacy.
9 Stores.
10 Bureaux.
11 Directeur.
12 Connecting Corridors.
13 Staircase.
14 Lingerie.

2nd Floor.

Centre Pavilion over the Chapel, the Bibliothèque.
Over the Refectories, the 'Salle de Chant' and the 'Salle de Jeu.'
Attics of main Building contain Workshops.
Infirmary Ward is in Court A.

number which diminishes materially the objections to corridors as a means of communication, provided they be ventilated with ordinary care. The whole suite of rooms on one side of a court of this building would hardly contain more beds than a single ward in a hospital. All the rooms are ventilated and warmed artificially on the usual Paris hospital method.

The plan consists simply of a number of separate rooms connected by a corridor, in which the convalescents sleep at night, while during the day they are out in the air, or following some occupation. The corridor construction, if properly ventilated, or, what is much better, if wholly or partially open, is not objectionable as a means of communication in a building of this kind intended for convalescents, who spend most of their time "out and about." For a hospital whose inmates are always confined to their wards, the structure would be objectionable.

This building, together with its economy, is worthy of careful examination by those engaged in planning convalescent establishments. It is, I believe, the largest building of the kind hitherto specially erected for the purpose. Of course, were it possible, it would be better to have more than one window for a bedroom to be occupied by three persons. And it would be highly advantageous if windows could be placed on two sides of the room.

The best arrangement of buildings for convalescents is, however, doubtless, that of a series of cottages; and here is a sketch of such a building (Plan No. 10) made at the request of the Committee for the Herbert memorial of the county of Wilts. It consists of four detached cottages, intended for twenty men and women. Two of the cottages are intended one for men and one for women. The centre cottage contains the sister's room, &c., together with two small wards for sick, or relapses, one for men and one for women. The fourth contains the kitchen and the men's and women's dining and day rooms.

It is intended to make the establishment as like a home and as unlike a hospital as possible, and to provide, at the same time, for strict discipline over the inmates.

A DESIGN FOR CONVALESCENT HOSPITAL ARRANGED AS COTTAGES.

PRINCIPAL ELEVATIONS.

1. *Dining and Day Room.*
2. *Kitchen.*
3. *Scullery.*
4. *Larder.*
5. *Stores.*
6. *Dispensary.*
7. *Maid Servants Room*
8. *Convalescent Bed Rooms*
9. *Sisters*
10. *Bath*
11. *Corridor*
12. *Covered Way*
13. *Gardener*
14. *Sick Wards*

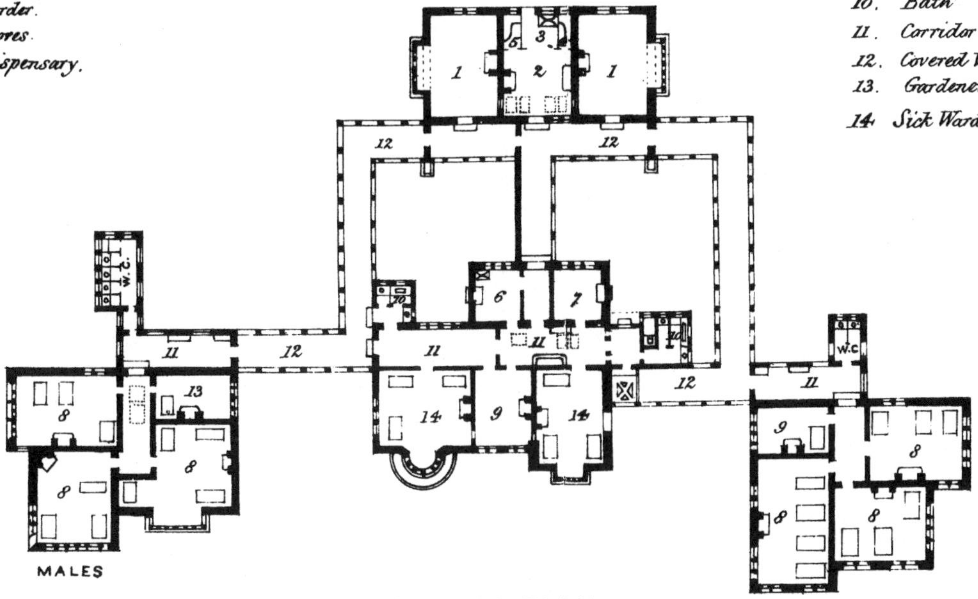

GROUND PLAN.

F. G. Netherclift, lith: 17 Mill Street, Conduit St.
London. Longman, Green & Co.

A plan such as this, while possessing all the advantages of a home, would admit of extension, merely by the addition of similar parts. The working plans were made by Mr. Thomas, of the War Office.

It is scarcely necessary to say that convalescent establishments should be placed in healthy, cheerful positions, varying in local climate according to the class of cases for which they are intended. The best climates can easily be determined by the usual practice adopted by physicians with private convalescents. Certain irritable chest cases do best in the moist relaxing sea-side climates of the S.W. of England. Diseases requiring a medium character of climate are usually sent to the southern districts, and to the Isle of Wight. If bracing sea-side climates are required, the S.E., E. and N.E. coasts and part of the N.W. coast are generally chosen. A large class of convalescents suffering from general constitutional debility are benefited by certain inland climates, such as Malvern, Clifton, Derbyshire, &c. I merely allude to this subject of climates because it should not be overlooked in providing for the relief of convalescents. There are many places round London on dry, comparatively elevated, gravelly soils, which would afford excellent sites for convalescent institutions.

If convalescent homes are necessary for adults, they are doubly necessary for children ; the rule, never to keep a patient a day longer in hospital than is absolutely essential, applies rather more to children than to any others.

It is necessary to say a few words on another proposal for convalescents—namely, providing convalescent wards and day-rooms in hospitals. In dealing with this proposal, it is right to repeat :—

1. That no patient should be kept in hospital a day longer than is absolutely essential—*i.e.*, for medical or surgical treatment.

2. That many, nay, most patients are quite unfit to return to a work-a-day life, even when they would be much better out of hospital. Where, then, should they go?

3. Every county and every hospital should have its convalescent branch, as unlike a hospital and as like a home as possible—best a string of cottages—where such can be received.

Do day-rooms in hospital answer this want? No. It is found practically impossible to keep such supervision over day-rooms as will prevent patients in them from playing tricks and from doing themselves more harm than good. Recovery has been found to be actually retarded by days in the day-rooms.

It has been suggested that a day-room should be attached to each ward, in order that patients in the day-room might be under the supervision of their own nurse. But the advantages of this supervision are more imaginary than real: practically a nurse can really supervise only as many persons as she can see from one point. Even in two wards in one line, and where everybody is in bed, an experienced nurse knows perfectly well how much really escapes her supervision. It would be doubly impossible for her to know what is going on in a day-room at the same time as in her ward, especially as it is quite out of the question that a day-room and ward should open out of one another. There might be one men's and one women's day-room for the whole hospital, with a head-nurse over each. But it is very undesirable to mix the patients of the several wards when they have to return to them. They meet only for gossip; they prefer this gossip to out-of-door exercise. And even if a head-nurse be spared—which she will not be—to manage them, she will succeed but with difficulty.

Practice differs widely from theory in these things. Practically it will be found that all patients, as long as they need to remain in hospital at all, had better be in their own wards, under their own nurse, provided those who *can* go out have as much out-of-door exercise as possible.

It has been objected that *no* ventilation can keep a sick ward fresh enough for semi-convalescents. Then how can it be fresh enough for sick?

It has been objected that semi-convalescents disturb the ward for serious cases. The serious cases, generally, think the ward very "dull" without them, and call a large, full ward "so cheerful."

In military hospitals it is totally different. For, 1. a soldier must either be in hospital or in barracks; 2. in a general hospital, a non-commissioned officer can always be placed over the day-room.

Do convalescent wards in hospital answer the want of a convalescent "home?" Certainly better than day-rooms; because convalescent wards are, or ought to be, always under a regular nursing staff, the same as sick wards are. But they would answer it much better still if they were totally out of and away from the hospital, in an institution of their own.

Convalescent wards are absolutely essential to a military hospital, especially in India; because you cannot send the semi-convalescent back to barracks, much less keep him in the fever and dysentery wards. Day and dining-rooms are also absolutely necessary for military convalescents, especially in India, if it were only for the plague of flies.

But day and dining-rooms are objectionable in a civil hospital. Taking the general run of cases, when patients can go into day and dining-rooms, they had better go out of hospital, not home, but into a convalescent institution. And even if there be none such to go to, their recovery and discharge from hospital is rather retarded than otherwise by day and dining-rooms.

Note on the Male Convalescent Hospital at Vincennes.

By Colonel Clark Kennedy, C.B.

1. Buildings.
2. The Convalescents, their Admission, Treatment, Diet, &c.
3. Administration.
4. General Remarks.

1. *Buildings.*—The 'Hospice Impérial des Invalides Civils' consists of a front of plain yet handsome elevation, with a central pavilion, forming the principal side of the Cour d'Honneur. On either flank of this front are three courts, two stories high, containing the wards for the convalescents and the connecting corridors, leaving the fourth side of the Cour d'Honneur open. The courts in a line with the central building, and extending backward, are connected by covered passages with a range of one-story offices placed in rear of the great central pavilion, thus forming two other courts, making in all eight courts, exclusive of the Cour d'Honneur. Continuations of the external lines of flank buildings give an elongated open space in front of the Cour d'Honneur, the whole laid out with turf plots, shrubs, &c., with a central basin and fountain. Gravel roads and walks are made, and the entrance from the lodge through the grounds is by what will be a handsome avenue. The entire grounds are a parallelogram, with the buildings placed about the centre, and comprise turfed recreation ground, gardens, large kitchen garden, and a considerable piece of the ground is left in the same condition as when the site was enclosed, with the trees and copse-wood still standing, so as to form a natural park, in which the convalescents are permitted to walk, except upon the days when friends are allowed to visit the inmates, when that part of the grounds is closed, in order to guard against the occurrence of irregularities.

The wards placed in two stories form the six flank courts; five wards compose the side of a court, and are entered from an enclosed corridor lighted by windows opposite to and corresponding to the door of each ward, the window of which is also in the same line. This construction allows a free current of air to be passed through each individual ward by opening the door and the two corresponding windows. Each ward is occupied by three convalescents, and is 19 feet 8 inches long, 12 feet 4 inches broad, and 9 feet 10 inches in height; giving about 800 cubic feet per man. The corridor is 5 feet 9 inches wide, and the same height. The lower two-thirds of the walls are painted in oil, the upper one-third in distemper. The flooring is of oak. There is neither stove nor fire-place, but warmth and ventilation are provided for on the down-draft system; the opening in the floor being about a foot square, and covered by a grating, that on the side of the wall being considerably smaller, and placed two or three feet above the flooring. Three iron bedsteads, with no curtains or hangings of any kind, with the usual circular springs in lieu of a paillasse (these appear to answer *admirably*), and a kind of commode cupboard with four partitions and a door to each, for the use of the inmates, formed the sole furniture.

A glance at the plan will show the excellent division of the courts into rows of wards and corridors, whereby the windows of one row of wards are in no case immediately opposite those of another.

The ground-floor of the central pavilion is the chapel, with the usual fitments, divided from the refectories on either side by moveable wooden partitions and thick curtains, which are drawn back when service is performed, and the congregation face inwards towards the altar.

Right and left of the chapel are the refectories—spacious, airy rooms, furnished with fourteen polished stone tables on iron legs, each accommodating sixteen people (seven on each side, and one at the two ends, if necessary); chairs are provided, and all meals, both of convalescents and the hospital servants, are taken in these rooms.

Behind the chapel, and communicating with both dining-rooms, are the kitchens; beneath them the cellars. The cooking apparatus and arrangements were good, but call for no remark, there being no novelty in them.

Directly in rear of the kitchens, and separated from them by the corridor connecting the two flank courts, was placed the laundry, the ironing-room, and a bath-room. The two former were in excellent working order, and fitted with the usual apparatus; but the bath-room was very small, and quite inadequate to the requirements of such an establishment as that at Vincennes.

The lavatories, situated in the courts, and fitted with basins, were good and sufficient, but they were only supplied with cold water.

The ground-floor of one side of No. 3 court is the pharmacy and stores, and the linen store is contained in a side of the court marked No. 4. This latter, in charge of the sisters, is beautifully kept; and I was struck with the great care taken in arranging the linen and clothing, so as to admit currents of air percolating through the piles, somewhat upon the principle of stacking deals for seasoning. This, although attended to in most stores, I had never seen carried to the same extent as it was here.

The second story of the central pavilion is a lofty, well-proportioned room, very handsomely fitted up as a library, and contains a collection of the best French works, presented to the institution by several of the leading booksellers in Paris. Newspapers are also taken in for use in the hospital. It is open daily from 12 noon till 4 P.M., and is much resorted to by the convalescents.

On the right of the library is a large apartment, the size of the refectory beneath, called the 'Salle de Chant,' fitted with an orchestra, music-stands, and benches for the audience, where vocal concerts are given every evening at seven o'clock, by the musical portion of the inmates, which not infrequently included singers of note in the musical world of Paris, whose necessities had led them to take advantage of the institution. These concerts were held most evenings, but no instrumental music ever appeared to be introduced.

The corresponding room on the left of the library is called the 'Salle de Jeu,' and is used as a day-room, fitted with tables, benches, and chairs. Smoking is here permitted, and an ample supply of dominoes, cards, chess, and draughts afforded objects of interest to all. Although the weather was fine, many of the tables were well filled. Several were walking up and down in conversation with each other; and some were seated at the windows, enjoying the bright and varied prospect of the woods, the environs, and the city of Paris itself, which the upper story of the building afforded.

In the second floor of Court 3 the infirmary is situated, where the convalescents who relapse, or who, as is sometimes the case, contract fresh disease in the establishment, are treated. It consists of a single airy ward of 18 beds, and is furnished with screens to partition off cases if it should be necessary.

In the third story, or rather attics of the main building, the workshops of the establishment are placed, in which tools and materials are provided for the use of any one willing and able to work. Nothing is made for sale, but only to supply the wants of the hospital, not only with respect to new work, but also with repairs. There is no compulsion; each convalescent works or not, as it pleases him; if he works he receives pay at the uniform rate of 50 c. a-day, and the whole of the workshops are under the superintendence of a skilled officer of the establishment. As many as *one-fourth* of the number of inmates have occasionally availed themselves of the workshops at the same time, and under no circumstances are they ever empty.

The staircases throughout the buildings were numerous and convenient.

The latrines were not in any way remarkable; they were amply ventilated, but there being no general system of drainage, the 'tonneaux' (barrels each with a small opening covered by a lid when removed) in connexion with them were emptied whenever necessary. There was nothing offensive about them, but the weather was cool with a fresh breeze blowing.

The director and other officials stated that the principle of small wards for the convalescents, giving accommodation to three persons in each, answered well; they did not express any preference for a larger number, and said that during the four years the hospital had been open, it had worked satisfactorily, and not expensively in practice. It did not appear to me that any administrative advantage would arise from placing the convalescents in larger wards, such as arises from the large ward system in hospitals for disease.

2. *The Convalescents, their Admission, Treatment, Diet, &c. &c.*—No one is admitted to the hospital without a certificate of convalescence from some constituted medical authority, and payments are made of 50 c. a-day by members of benefit societies; 75 c. by those belonging to the large workshops, who subscribe at a certain rate; and 1 franc by those able to pay towards their own support. These three classes are not, however, so numerous as the fourth class, who pay nothing, and are admitted free upon certificates from the medical men of the Paris hospitals in which they have been treated.

All religions and sects are alike allowed to participate in the benefits of the hospital.

The stage of recovery which may be considered as convalescence can hardly be defined, but as a general rule no one confined to bed, no one requiring nursing, or unable to walk, or take his share in the usual duties of keeping his ward in good order, would be eligible. No consumptive patients are ever admitted in any stage of their complaints.

When a convalescent relapses, or falls ill, he is treated in the infirmary as he would be in a hospital, either until his recovery, his death, or arrival at such a state of health as to justify his return to a hospital, or to being placed in a poor-house. The per-centage of deaths is very trifling, but I am unable to state it.

The rate of payment in no way affects the treatment of the individual, all fare alike.

The treatment appeared to be very simple; few drugs, airy rooms, good beds, sufficient clothing, a liberal and varied diet, rest for the weary, and the means of occupation and amusement provided, but forced upon no one; thus gently stimulating both mind and body to enable them to regain their tone.

The surveillance exercised over the inmates is only sufficient to preserve order and regularity; and as much individual freedom of action (such as remaining in-doors, going into the grounds, reading, playing, &c. &c.) was permitted as possible.

The rank in life of the convalescents appeared to include all classes between the lower grades of traders and shopkeepers, and the workman, or labourer, who lives by weekly or daily wages. Struggling artists, actors, and musicians, are not the least frequent inmates. I do not think that the actual pauper is often admitted, and although not absolutely excluded, appears to be virtually so—but upon this point I am not certain.

There is no fixed time for the stay of convalescents in the establishment; occasionally they have been discharged after three or four days, and others have remained as many months; but the director states that from twenty-one to twenty-three days may be considered as the average duration of stay. Any unusual case, or one where the medical officer is of opinion that health will not be restored, is reported to the Minister of the Interior, and the patient is either returned to his friends, a hospital, or a hospice. Should, however, the convalescence be tedious and lingering, the patient is never discharged, however long the period may be.

Under peculiar circumstances the inmates are permitted to leave the establishment for a few hours, but that is rare. Friends are admitted on three days a week after 12 noon. Patients under 15 years of age are not professedly admitted, but the rule is not absolute, and lads of 11 and 12 are often received.

Each man upon admission gives his own clothing into store, and receives a shirt, a pair of socks (either cotton or woollen according to the season), towel, napkin, pocket-handkerchief, pair of sheets, pillow case, dark blue loose coat and trousers of soft woollen cloth; in summer, blouse and trousers of light material. Pair of boots for out-door wear, and slippers with thick hemp soles, such as are worn in the Pyrenees, for use in the house. In winter, a cloth cap; in summer, a straw hat. Should it be wished to wear their own under-clothing it is allowed; but the wearing the cap, coat, and trousers is compulsory.

The sheets are changed once a month, and the personal linen weekly. No article, however short a time in use, is ever re-issued without being thoroughly cleansed, even the linen lining of the caps and straw hats is unpicked and washed.

The clothing and bedding is suitable and sufficient.

The diet roll hangs up in the kitchen, and is so arranged that the diet of no two consecutive days is exactly alike. The dietary not being adapted to English habits of life, I did not take a copy; but it consisted of soups, meat, vegetables, eggs, cheese, and biscuits, together with the allowance of ½ litre of most excellent wine (Burgundy), and bread at discretion.

The meal hours are 7½, 10½ A.M., and 5 P.M. On any particular day, such as the Fête Napoleon, coffee is given as a treat.

The director mentioned that when the establishment was first opened, a very ample allowance of bread was made to each individual, but seeing both dissatisfaction and waste, he made the allowance unlimited, and the result has been a very large saving, so considerable as to amount to an item of some importance. (I can verify this from my own experience with troops on board ship, and on service.)

In cases where any extra or peculiar diet is considered necessary, it is given without hesitation.

Should any one wish to change his ward, or the table in the refectory to which he had been told off, in order to be with a friend or acquaintance, permission is at once granted.

3. *The Administration.*—The administration consists of 63 persons, *vide* the annexed list procured in the hospital. I need not enlarge upon their individual duties, as the names of the offices they hold will point them out.

The physician does *not* reside in the establishment, but makes his visits from Paris. The three 'internes' are always on the spot. The duties of the infirmary are kept distinct from those of the rest of the establishment, and one sister, assisted by four 'infirmiers,' nurse the sick.

The whole of the linen and clothing is in charge of two other sisters; both that for the convalescents, and for the employés of the hospital. Eight women, hired by the day, perform the work of the laundry and of the mending-room.

Service Administratif.

1 Directeur.	2 Employés de bureaux (ordinaires).
1 Receveur-econome.	1 Architecte.
3 Employés de bureaux (supérieurs).	1 Inspecteur des travaux.

Service de Santé.

1 Médecin.	3 Internes.

Culte.

1 Aumônier.	6 Religieuses.

Services Divers.

1 Surveillant-chef.	1 Gazier Lampiste.
3 Sous-surveillants.	1 Perruquier barbier.
1 Garde-magasins.	1 Garçon de salubrité.
1 Garçon de bureau.	5 Garçons de galeries.
1 Garçon de chantier.	1 Garçon de bains.

Services Divers—continued.

1 Concierge.	2 Cochers.
1 Cuisinier-chef.	1 Mécanicien.
1 Aide-cuisinier.	2 Chauffeurs.
1 Sommelier.	1 Menusier.
1 Aide-sommelier.	1 Serrurier.
1 Réfectorier.	1 Tailleur.
3 Laveurs de vaisselle.	1 Jardinier-chef.
1 Garçon de pharmacie.	1 Aide-jardinier.
1 Tisannier.	1 Buandier.
4 Infirmiers.	1 Repasseuse.

The 'employés' are rationed and clothed by the hospital, and take their meals in the refectories at hours subsequent to the meal times of the convalescents.

The number of servants employed is ample to perform the work, for the wards are cleaned, swept out, beds made, &c., by the convalescents themselves; the three inmates of each ward taking the duty in turn whenever their condition will allow them to do so. Some assist in the garden and grounds, others in the kitchen, and cellar, &c., but the only compulsory work performed was that of the care of their respective wards.

Most of the linen, and some of the clothing used in the hospital is made in the Salpêtrière, the work of one establishment assisting to support the other.

The director informed me that the entire cost of the hospital averaged for each convalescent the sum of 2 fs. 40 c. per diem.

The hospital is supported by the State, although private individuals have made considerable donations to the funds.

The establishment is under the direction of the Minister of the Interior, as well as the Female Convalescent Hospital at Vesinet, and they are neither of them within the control of the 'Assistance Publique;' having a separate office for their management.

4. *General Remarks.*—The site is good; the air fresh; and the soil sandy; but nevertheless there must be some defect with respect to the drainage of the foundations, for in many places the walls within a few feet of the ground were unmistakeably damp. With the exception of the cellarage, there is no basement story.

The latrines might be improved; and the bathing accommodation was unworthy of the name, being most scanty.

The cleanliness of the buildings and grounds, the freshness of the wards, and the entire absence of the peculiar odour which hangs about most buildings occupied by invalids, were satisfactory.

I did not visit the establishment in wet or close weather, therefore I am unable to speak as to how the ventilation would work with closed doors and windows. There was no rain during my short visit to Paris.

The administration appeared to be conducted upon the common-sense principle, and after-reflection has only confirmed me in the opinion I formed on the spot, that the success or failure of a convalescent hospital would mainly depend upon the good judgment and moral influence of the director or governor. Upon him the whole onus must rest whether it becomes a prey to schemers and a receptacle of the dead weight of other hospitals in the form of impracticable or incurable patients, or, as great a benefit as can be conferred, restoring strength to the friendless and needy newly risen from their sick beds.

Having seen Vincennes, I am satisfied that with care in the choice of instruments, a convalescent hospital may be made an institution of much value, and an excellent supplement to other existing hospitals.

April, 1861.

VI.

CHILDREN'S HOSPITALS.

THE first thing to decide is whether you will have a children's hospital at all. On the one hand, none but the hospital-experienced can possibly guess how important public opinion is to keep a hospital in any way straight. Ay, even with the best religious order for nurses. Now, among children, there can be no public opinion. They cannot make their complaints; and even if they do, it is always unwise for doctors or visitors to take part with the children against the nurses, who are always with them, and ought to be in authority over them. And the nurses will take their revenge (and cannot help doing so) upon the children. For certainly the children are not in authority over *them*. Also, each sick child may almost be said to require a nurse to itself. Where adults are mixed with them, the woman in the next bed, if the patients are judiciously distributed, often becomes the child's best protector and nurse. And it does her as much good as it does the child. It is a matter of universal hospital experience that this intermingling of ages is essential. Let the age of admission be, at all events, raised so as to include 15 years, especially on the female side, if you decide on a children's hospital. To have the best religious order as nurses, does not at all guarantee the child-patient from, at least, indifference, since there is a tacit idea among some "religious" that it is better for the children to die than to live. Indeed, more tenderness has been shown to them sometimes among the commonest hospital nurses. It is not enough to be merely conscientious and patient with sick children. There must be a real genuine vocation and love for the work; a feeling as if your own happiness were bound up in each particular child's recovery. Nothing else will carry you through the perpetual wear and tear to the spirits, of the fretfulness, the unreasonableness of sick children—not that I think it is greater than that of many sick adults—but it is more wearing, because the strain is never off you for a minute. This hearty love of and companionship with sick children, such as the Wilderspins felt for their *well* pupils, is essential for a nurse in a children's hospital. It is to be found just as often and just as seldom among mothers as among nuns. The true *maternal* feeling may be in the girl and the old maid. But wherever it is, there only must the good nurse for children be looked for. Duty and conscience must come in too, of course, because no natural feeling will stand the fatigue and anxiety always.

These are the peculiarities of children's hospitals, to be weighed before such are decided upon. Shall you find nurses sufficient of this kind?

The only idea of many (doctors and others) about a child's hospital is that it is a place where children are to be admitted and to be recovered, or dead and buried as soon as possible. Such is not our idea.

But, whatever you do, do not have children's wards in a general hospital. There at least mix up the children with the adults. For a children's ward in a general hospital combines all the disadvantages with none of the advantages of a children's hospital.*

On the other hand, the advantages of a children's hospital are that there they do not see the things which they had much better not see, and which it is impossible to prevent their seeing in an adult hospital, and that children's hospitals require and obtain far larger recreation and exercise grounds and more appliances, than hospitals for adults.

Paris exhibits and London does not what is justly thought necessary in this respect. Physical exercises in and out of doors are a part of the treatment, in all but acute cases. So is teaching, secular as well as religious. So is bathing.

It must never be forgotten that children can never be left alone for a moment—and that a separate staff must be provided for every room—I had almost said a nurse for every child.

The bathing establishment forms a most important branch of a children's hospital. In all children's hospitals abroad, the classification is

1. Medical.
2. Surgical.
3. Cutaneous.

And in all continental hospitals the proportion of the cutaneous is large.

I speak of the Continent, because England, indeed, affords no large experience as to children's hospitals.

---

* There are, besides, certain children's habits, which I can do no more than allude to here, perfectly well known to all who have had much to do with children's wards, which render the strictest supervision necessary; and this is much more likely to be obtained in a special children's hospital, all under the same responsible management, and with every special means of treatment and exercise and occupation, than in any children's wards in a general hospital, where sick children are only received and dealt with as a portion of the hospital inmates, yet without the protection and amusement of being with the "big" inmates.

The bathing establishment must, therefore, consist of four separate bathing places.

1 for boys
2 ,, cutaneous
3 for girls
4 ,, cutaneous.

And neither sex should ever come on the side appropriated to the other.

Each bathing-place must be under the charge of a separate competent "sister," with one or more attendants under her; otherwise the lists of accidents, by drownings and scaldings alone, will be fearful.

Each bathing-place must have a number of small baths, separable by a curtain or slight partition, with one or more large baths, in which several children may be bathed at once.

The girls must bathe alone; the infants together, unless the disease is something special.

The medical officers must decide when the age comes when boys should bathe alone.

Girls should always be bathed in frocks, unless the special disease prevents it.

Out-door patients are always (to their own great advantage and to the in-patients' great disadvantage) admitted to baths and gymnastics in these institutions.

This must be taken into account.

In regard to the water-closets, as a general rule, there should be no possibility for a child to fasten itself in, or to communicate with another child when in. They should be self-acting, and well lighted day and night.

It is almost needless to say that the lavatories for children must not be lavatories for adults, as to height, handiness, or anything else, and that the children who will have to be washed in ward are much more numerous than adults in hospital, consequently there must be a much greater provision of portable basins, &c. On this point foreign hospitals are wofully deficient. To prevent a child's skin from becoming chafed (in certain diseases) it has to be partially sponged many times a day.

The bath-room at the end of each large ward should contain two small baths, for acute cases or infants. There should also be a portable bath.

A large garden-ground, laid out in sward and grass hillocks, and such ways as children like (*not too pretty* for the children to be scolded for spoiling it) must be provided—or rather four such grounds for

1. Boys
2. ,, cutaneous
3. Girls
4. ,, cutaneous.

These must be combined with gymnastic grounds and halls *in* and *out of* doors.

A professor (a man) must be attached to superintend these exercises; otherwise the children, especially the girls, will injure themselves.

I have already said that out-patients are always admitted to these, which form a very important part of the treatment.

Singing in chorus should accompany some exercises.

A "sister" must superintend each of the play-grounds, besides the professor for all.

The gymnastic covered place may also be used as a play room and day-room, and as a school-room.

In foreign children's hospitals two school-rooms—one for boys and one for girls—are generally attached. And these again are each under the charge of a "sister," who teaches—

besides the teaching in the wards and the teaching by the chaplain.

The chapel should be contrived so that secular as well as religious teaching may be conducted there by the chaplain. Boys and girls may sit on opposite sides of the chapel. This is the only place where they should meet.

Special care should be taken to occupy the children enough, and only enough, to conduce to their recovery. Prizes and suchlike incentives may be given.

All experienced children's doctors lay immense stress upon this:—viz., that *every* child's hospital ought to have *a convalescent* branch at a distance, in the most healthy spot that can be found—probably by the sea, or at a watering-place. And this, however munificently the hospital itself may be furnished with air and exercise.

In all hospitals (in a child's hospital much more than in others) the patient must not stay a day longer than is absolutely necessary.

Finally, I must remark that the perfection of all these arrangements abroad, and the obstinate mortality of the children, are equally remarkable. Sometimes an epidemic disease will sweep a whole ward. One child out of five has actually died (from 1804 to 1861 inclusive) at the "Enfans Malades" at Paris, the greatest and oldest child's hospital in the world.

The only plan of a children's hospital which realizes all the various conditions laid down, is that to be erected at Lisbon, of which here is a sketch (No. 11). This plan possesses peculiar interest, on account of its being the embodiment of a desire of the late King of Portugal, to commemorate his lost queen.

Our own beloved Albert, who is always present in the longing and grateful recollection of Her Majesty's faithful subjects, had every stage of the plan brought to him, and made constant suggestions—it being his anxious wish to introduce into Portugal in a model building all the recent improvements in hospital construction made in this country. The architect was Mr. Humbert, to whom the design was entrusted by the Prince Consort.

The building is arranged along a parallelogram, 135 feet long by 75 feet wide, surrounded by an open corridor and terrace. It consists of two pavilions, similar in construction to those of the Lariboisière. These pavilions are two floors in height, and the upper wards are reached by wide open staircases. One peculiarity of the pavilion is, that the nursing staff is all accommodated in the staircase end of it. This is effected simply by putting an additional floor at the top of the staircase. Each ward contains thirty-two beds. The water-closets, bath, and lavatory, are at the farther end of the long wards. They are specially planned for children's use. Each closet is ventilated separately, and is also cut off from the body of the compartment in which it is placed, so that all of them are surrounded by a considerable mass of constantly moving air passing through the compartment by windows on three sides, *in addition to* a window for each separate closet. If any foul air were by chance to escape from the closet, notwithstanding its ventilation, into the compartment, the foul air would at once be mingled with a large body of moving air, and carried outside the building. Escape of foul air into the ward is thus rendered impossible. Each large ward is provided with two small baths, children's size, having hot and cold water laid on. Each ward is 128 feet long, by 30 feet wide, and 18 feet high, and gives 2160 cubic feet per bed. They will be the most magnificent wards in Europe. There are nine windows and one fireplace on each side. Besides the

PLAN OF CHILDREN'S HOSPITAL. LISBON.

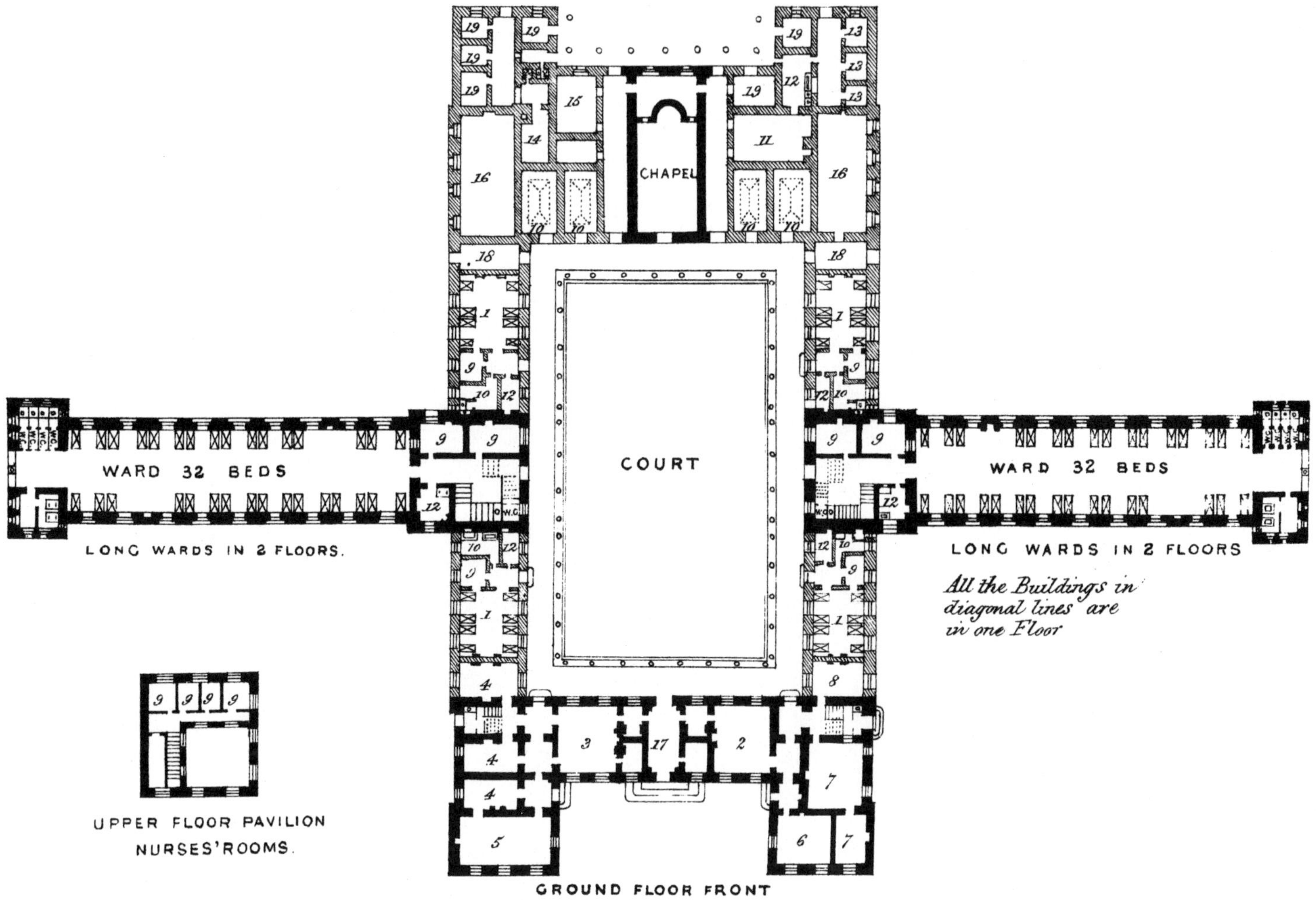

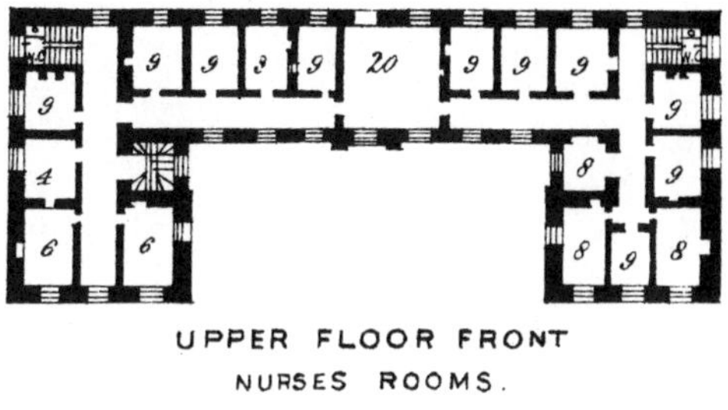

1. Small Wards
2. Board Room
3. Dispensary
4. Physician & Surgeon
5. Out Patients
6. Director
7. Clean Linen & Mending Rooms
8. Matron
9. Nurses' Rooms
10. Baths
11. Kitchen
12. Scullery
13. Larder, &c.
14. Heating Chamber
15. Operation Room
16. Convalescent Day Room
17. Vestibule
18. Passage
19. Stores
20. Nurses' Dining Room

F. G. Nethercift lith 17 Mill Street Conduit St. W
London Longman, Green & Cº

wards in the pavilions, there are four small wards of eight beds each, placed on the sides of the court. They are provided with nurses' rooms, scullery, water-closet, &c. The front of the hospital contains the administrative offices, and quarters for the director, medical officer, matron and sisters not attached to the beds. This part is two floors in height. The chapel is placed as in the Lariboisière plan, and on each side of it are the general baths of the establishment. In this same part of the hospital are two day-rooms, also kitchen, stores, and other offices.

It will be observed that the only buildings which exceed one floor in height are the administration, the two pavilions, and the chapel. And although there is a closed court, the sides of the court consist essentially of one floor buildings. The general bathing arrangements, day-rooms, and exercising grounds, are all made in conformity with the principles already stated. Taken as a whole, the building has been well considered in its details, and will, no doubt, prove a healthy structure.

If children's hospitals are to be built at all, this is the kind of plan that should be adopted. But every variation from it will require as much careful consideration as was bestowed on the original plan.

NOTE ON THE ATTENDANCE REQUIRED IN CHILDREN'S HOSPITALS.

If the nurses' quarters ought to be separate in a military hospital, certainly the men's ought to be separate in a child's hospital.

Not one woman more than is absolutely essential ought to be in a military hospital. Not one man more than is absolutely necessary ought to be in a children's hospital.

The only men who ought to sleep in a child's hospital are—

1. Resident medical officer (supposed to be a man of weight and experience).
2. Porter (who should be as far off the wards as possible).

The director (or whatever he may be called) and the chaplain (if this is conformable with the usage of the clergy) are the only other men who may sleep in the building.

The cook and her assistants should be women.

Women must be in undisputed charge of a child's hospital, saving, of course, as above said, the direction and the medical service.

On the Continent, where men do far more of household work than with us, the necessity of having as few men as possible in children's hospitals is fully recognised.

All cleaning, which *must* be done by men, should be done by men not attached to the hospital.

No male attendants must ever be attached to children's wards.

A children's hospital requires far more attendants than an adult hospital. All must be women; and all ought to sleep near their respective wards.

The two schoolmistresses are the only women who need not live in the hospital.

Reverent decency in the dead-house, so much neglected in England, is peculiarly desirable in children's hospitals. It should be a separate building in a quiet corner, beyond the possibility of being overlooked, with two separate entrances, one into the *post mortem* room, the other opening from the outer wall, for the relations to come in.

VII.

INDIAN MILITARY HOSPITALS.

The Report, Evidence, and Stational Reports issued by the Royal Commission on the sanitary state of the Indian army, contain a large amount of exceedingly interesting information as to the condition of military and female hospitals in that part of the empire, the results of which I purpose to give, with the view of deducing from the inquiry principles which might be applied in future hospital buildings for Indian climates.

The Indian hospitals, though planned on simple principles, admitting of admirable details, are, as a rule, exceedingly bad as regards points considered essential to health and administration, even in this country. What would be, *e.g.*, thought in this country of a hospital without a water-closet, or bath, or means of personal cleanliness? Such a hospital would be considered as a mere makeshift, till accommodation fitter for recovery could be provided.

The "means of ablution" in Indian hospitals are often "a tin pot, with which the sick pour the water over themselves." Or, as at Bombay, they "take water to bathe themselves from a trough." Elsewhere, they have "one tub, one basin, to 100 men." The means of washing, as at Ramandroog, a convalescent station, are "two shallow earthenware pie-dishes," "on a form in a room" ("very chilly in damp" weather) "adjoining where the night-stools are."

At Rangoon the "bathing accommodation" is "hitherto nothing but a tub of water, without basin, soap, or towel."

There may be a bath-room. But "all apparatus is entirely wanting." The sick "can always, if they please, get a skin-full of water thrown over them by the water-carriers," as at Hazareebaugh.

One may safely say that when the sick are able to bathe in India, it is a sufficient test of their being able to leave hospital, as has indeed been discovered to be the case at some home stations.

At Nynee Tal the sick bathe in the lake. Darjeeling says, "in fact, the inducements to remain dirty are, especially in the case of sickly men, greater than those to be clean."

There does not appear to be a single well-placed orderlies' or nurses' room in any of the hospitals, from which the sick can be seen at all times, and where the nurses themselves can be inspected. The surgeon's and "nurses'" quarters are sometimes three-quarters of a mile or a mile off, so that they (the medical and nursing attendants) are represented as spending their whole day in going backwards and forwards on the road.

The hospital is generally surrounded by a "high prison-like wall." At Ghazeepore it is said, "of course all the buildings generally are most unsuitable for hospital purposes." Proper ventilation is represented, as at Baroda, as "next to impossible." At Kolapore the rain beats in through the cowls, and "makes the wards so damp that charcoal has to be used to dry them." The water for drinking may be brought, as at Bangalore, from a tank which receives the whole sewage of the cantonment, and which "just now is not very clean," from which "hundreds of bullock loads of impure matter are removed year after year when the tank is low and the smell from it most offensive." Or the water may be brought (cholera also being brought with it) from wells into which the said tank drains. The drainage may be by an open ditch into the tank, whence the hospital derives its water. Or the water supply may, perhaps, have to be carried from half a mile off, or even from two miles off, as at Madras. But " no improvement is required in this respect." (!) The privies are everywhere either " highly offensive" or " not more offensive than the best of such places usually are in this country." Or the privies are " without seats," and are " kept pure by burning salt in them." " Arrangements admit of improvement."

Scarcely ever is there any provision of separate wards for convalescents; although, in a country whose scourge is dysentery, to leave men convalescing from dysentery in the same place and under the same circumstances as those suffering from dysentery, is just to ensure as far as possible their *not* convalescing. The same may be said of fever and of bowel diseases generally. Convalescents pass their whole 24 hours in bed, except during their time of exercise (*where* they have means of exercise) on elephants, in sick carts, or doolies. They have not even a room to take their meals in, but eat their food upon their knees, sitting on their beds, "possibly with dying men around;" or they are sent to barracks and put on barrack rations, and " marched out under a non-commissioned officer morning and evening for exercise."

Where there is no guard-house the " men on guard occupy a corner of the hospital verandah, where they eat, drink, and smoke at their discretion." No hospitals have dining-rooms, although all ought to have them because of the pest of flies in India. Not one has a day-room for men who can leave their beds.

The " sanitary state" is generally represented as " good," although at the same time we are told as in certain cases that the hospital is "unfit for accommodation of European patients;" or that "epidemic disease has appeared in it;" that "sores become erysipelatous;" that, as at Bangalore, "one of the flags" in the floor being removed, "the smell from the opening was so offensive that" the surgeon was "obliged to run;" that "gangrene and phagedæna have appeared, when the hospital was crowded;" that the "privy is a nuisance to one ward;" that the "cesspools are always more or less offensive;" or that the "outhouses are in a very dirty and unwashed condition." At Muttra the contents of the latrines are "carted away every morning for combustion in one of the many brick-kilns which surround the station, and help to poison the air." At Madras the "sanitary state" is called "good," and the commander-in-chief himself adds, "if the vile, stinking river Kooum were not under the very noses of the patients." Both cholera and gangrene have appeared at times in the hospital. The latrines are placed to windward "unfortunately;" "tubs only are used." The privy is washed daily, and charcoal "burned in it." It is called "not offensive," the commander-in-chief again adding, "a year ago it was odiously offensive."

No wonder it is stated, as at Bangalore, that "sick men are reluctant to come into hospital from barracks," and that the medical officer does not want "convalescent wards," because he finds it better to send his convalescents to barracks, where they recover faster.

From some hospitals the "impurities" are removed by hand carriage to 30 yards from the hospital. In another, the privy is said to be a "disgrace to the 19th century." One wonders to what century it would be a credit.

At most hospitals the bedsteads are of wood instead of iron, and the men break them to pieces in their "efforts to expel the vermin." As at Ramandroog, where men are sent for their health, "the building swarms with bugs." And so of every barrack and hospital where these wooden bedsteads are used. One surgeon complains of the serious injury to his sick occasioned by want of sleep from vermin. The bedding is of hemp or straw, instead of hair. Hair it ought always to be in hospitals, and hair is now the regulation in all Queen's hospitals. It appears from several reports that sheets are not provided except for dysentery and fever: and certainly in no hospital deserving the name should the Inspector-general feel himself called on to recommend that "a good mattress, a blanket, *sheets*, and pillow-cases should be provided for every bed," as does the excellent Inspector-general of the Madras Presidency.

Figs. 27, 28, are illustrations of the smaller class of regi-

FIG. 27.

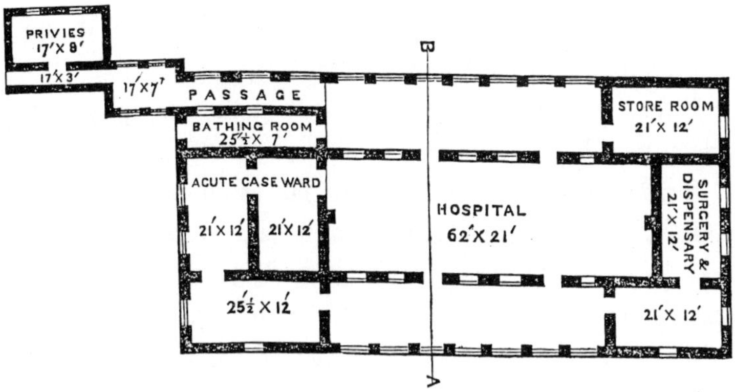

Plan and Elevation of Horse Artillery Hospital, Bangalore.

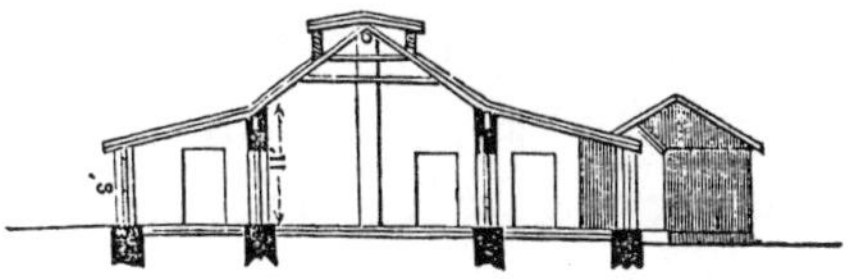

Section on A B.

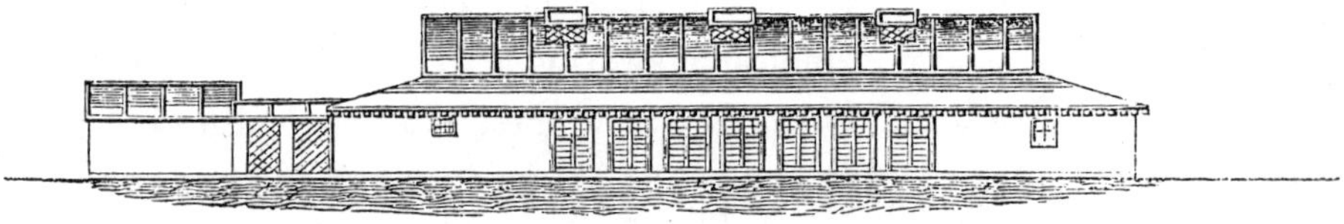

Horse Artillery Hospital, Bangalore.

mental (British) hospitals. Fig. 27 shows the simpler form of construction, a single large ward, partially enclosed by other rooms for sick, all communicating and having a common ventilation, the arrangement good and simple up to a certain point, and then marred in the details. There are privies in place of water-closets, with covered passages, to conduct foul air to the sick in certain states of the wind. Bangalore gives a reason for "the covered way to the latrines," which we never should have thought of. It is a "covered place for exercise."

It will be seen that the hospital is entirely destitute of proper ward offices.

Fig. 28 shows a somewhat better construction of hospital, but there is the same defect in detail.

Either plan might answer for temporary camp purposes, in default of better, but that is all.

Indian hospitals generally, so far as all conveniences and comforts are concerned, appear to be simply camp hospitals; good, because the best possible for field service, but by no means good or the best possible for permanent stations.

There is no instance, except at Wellington, where the hospital, if on one floor, as is usual, is raised from the ground with any current of air beneath. These hospitals are stated, as at Bangalore, to be "always damp in wet weather." And often the floor is merely the ground bricked over. Rangoon and Tonghoo live like the beavers, and raise their barracks and hospitals on piles, with free passage for air underneath. The

Fig. 28.

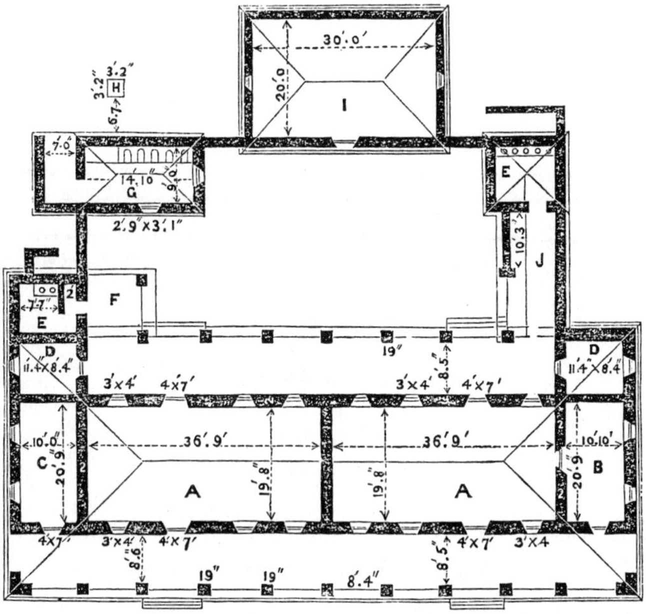

Plan and Elevation of Artillery Hospital, Belgaum.

consequence is, that in those jungly swamps, they are more healthy than at most other Indian stations where the men sleep close to the ground.

As at Allahabad, Barrackpore, Dinapore, Meerut, Kurrachee, and Secunderabad, vast wards of from 100 to 150 beds, and even up to more than 200 beds, exactly the same as the barrack-rooms, are in use.

Here is a plan and section of one ward at Dinapore, which is nothing but a passage 633 feet long with 150 beds in it.

FIG. 29.

Plan and Section of Hospital, Dinapore

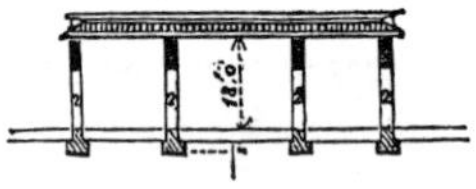

The wards can never be said to be light or airy; "as a general rule, hospitals are badly lighted and gloomy;" doors are more common than windows. And these doors, when closed, leave the ward, if not absolutely dark, yet absolutely dismal and close. Indeed a dark ward must always be a close ward. Or "light enters from a couple of panes in the doors near the top, and when closed darkness is almost complete." There is in Indian hospitals hardly a room light enough to perform a surgical operation. And operations, it is stated, have to be performed in verandahs.

The inner verandahs are generally used for sick wherever more room is wanted: the outer ones sometimes cut up for lavatories, destroying what ventilation there is.

The superficial area per bed is almost invariably too small, and the wards almost as invariably too high; the result to the sick being that, with an apparently sufficient cubic space, the surface overcrowding is excessive. One of the worst examples of this is the recently constructed hospital at Trimulgherry

(Secunderabad), which consists of three wards, two of which contain no fewer than 228 beds each; the wards are 42 feet high, and afford 1001 cubic feet per bed, but the surface area

FIG. 30.

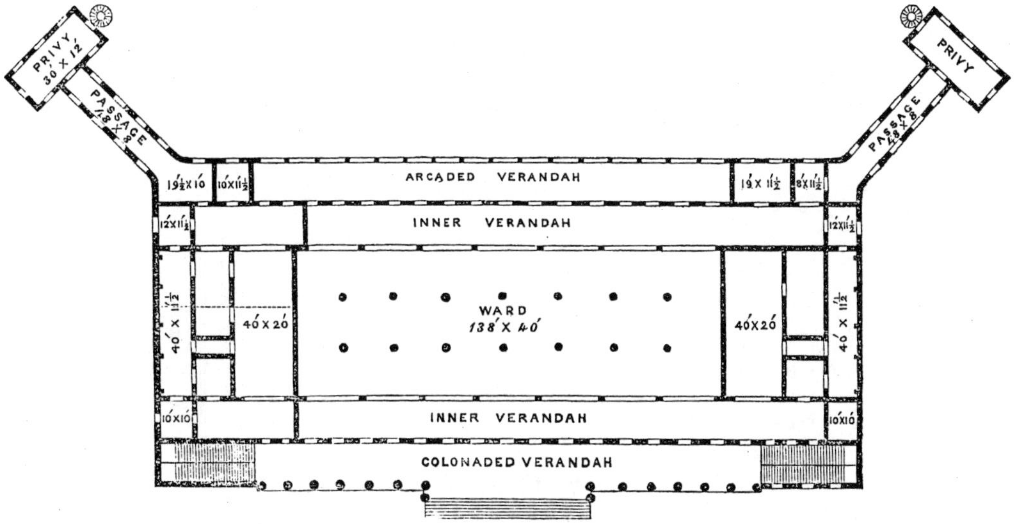

Plan of Hospital Ward, Trimulgherry (Secunderabad). 228 Beds.

per bed is only 24 square feet. This surface overcrowding is greater than I have ever seen it in the smallest or the largest temporary war hospitals. Such facts strike one very forcibly in connexion with the high mortality among sick entering these and similar hospitals.

This Trimulgherry hospital is an immense hall supported on pillars and arches, and the surface crowded with beds. The distance from outer air to outer air, free of the building, is about 80 feet.

The general hospital at Madras is constructed on a different principle from any others, but on as bad an one. It consists of a centre and two wings, and appears to be intended for four rows of beds between the opposite doors and windows.

FIG. 31.

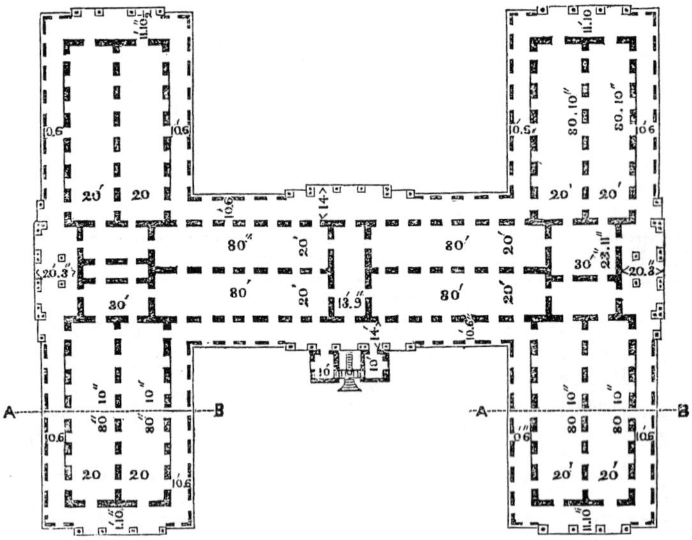

Plan and Section of General Hospital, Fort St. George, Madras.

Section on A B.

All the sanitary defects of barracks re-appear and with worse consequences in the hospitals: viz., bad water-supply, bad ventilation, no drainage, (Ferozepore says, "drainage not necessary,") offensive latrines, so offensive indeed that the patients have sometimes to leave a particular ward, no means of bathing, and hardly any of cleanliness.

There are besides, however, two grave defects not felt in barracks, but peculiar and fatal to hospitals.

These are the cooking and the attendance. It is in several reports complained that under the present system the cooks (natives or Portuguese), are nothing but "miserable pretenders," because the pay is so small; that the kitchens are no better than, but just the same as the barrack kitchens. They are often small open sheds, without chimneys, the smoke finding its way out as it can, and with but few utensils; sometimes the food is prepared on the ground. "But we are accustomed to this in India." It is added, that though common food is tolerably well prepared, there is nothing whatever that can be called sick cookery, nothing whatever to tempt the appetite or spare the digestion of the sick man, whom the hospital is for.

In hospitals at home, trained cooks of the army hospital corps are now in charge of the cooking, under the direction of the purveyor, who is responsible that the diets are properly cooked. In India the chief quality in native cooks appears to be the "pursuit of cooking under difficulties;" their ingenuity in bringing about an *apparently* good result, in a rude and often bad way, is frequently admired by the reporters, as if the end of cooking were "to make a pair of old boots look like a beefsteak."

In England where the grass-fed meat is so much better than in India, it is found necessary to put the purveying of meat for hospitals under the charge of the purveyor, for the sake of always obtaining the best quality.

There does not appear to be any provision of this kind in India, where all is under the commissariat.

As to the attendants, they are just the same as would be supplied to idle healthy men. Quantity, it would seem, is supposed to supply quality. In serious cases a "waiting man" is supplied "from the battalion, who is relieved daily."

That is, he goes on guard for 24 hours, as in the guard-room, so in the sick-room. It appears that mounting guard in the sick-room is disliked, and the guard sometimes neglects his patient.

As to supposing that any nursing is required, the thing is totally out of the question. There are neither trained orderlies nor female nurses.

A matron is sometimes "sanctioned," but "only for a complete battalion." If there are fewer sick they must do without. Every severe case, as has been stated, is allowed to have its comrade to itself in from the ranks, *i.e.*, the case which requires the best nursing is to have the worst nurse. Something more is needed to make a nurse, as well as a surgeon, than mere kindness. Wherever the above comrade-practice is found, we know beforehand that there can be no nursing, no discipline in that hospital, and any amount of drink.

There is generally one hospital sergeant and a "plentiful supply of ward coolies." The hospital sergeant is for discipline, and under him are 79 coolies and bheesties in cold weather, 240 in hot weather. This for an European corps. The general impression, as regards the native attendants,* is that they are in some sense kind, but "as a rule, very inattentive," and when there is any pressure of sick they are "lazy," and "apathetic," and the sick, it need hardly be said, neglected, and "averse to be waited on by them." When at

* And here comes in again the difficulty of difference in language. Our men dislike and despise the natives, and are regarded by them in return more as wild beasts than fellow-creatures. The native, however, makes much more effort to learn the Briton's language than does the Briton to learn the native's. It is difficult to give an idea of the evil effects of the gross ignorance of all that relates to the country in the ranks of our army in India. The commonest attempt at conversation gives rise to feelings of impatience and irritation, too often followed by personal ill-treatment. Where the Briton is sick, it is of course worse.

a hill station, as Landour, the hospital sergeant is taken at random from the sick men themselves, sent up for convalescence; it is needless to point out the consequences. This grievance has been repeatedly represented, but in vain.

Nynee Tal has one hospital sergeant, one barber, one orderly, for its attendance.

Lady Canning introduced female nurses at Allahabad, who are mentioned (in the Stational Return of Allahabad) as being a great comfort to the sick. Wherever there are general hospitals there should be female nurses, but only under the organization laid down by the Medical Regulations of October 1859. It is a great mistake to put down a few women among a parcel of men (orderlies and patients) without exactly defining the women's duties and place.

Lastly, there appears nowhere in India to be provided any means of drying hospital linen, even during the rains. It is often complained that the washing is very bad and that the native washermen tear the linen, and at one cavalry hospital this keeps two tailors constantly employed in repairing the rents and injuries; for native washing is done by beating the linen against large flat stones or wooden boards.

If the British military hospitals are such, what must be said of those for our native troops? Here the patients "diet *themselves*."

Native Hospitals.—As regards construction, where native hospitals have been specially built, they resemble the smaller class of British hospital. One of the most complete of these is shown in fig. 32. There are wards within wards, completely enclosed by other rooms, of which, although there are plenty, not one is suited for ward offices.

But it must not be supposed that native hospitals are all as good as this. They are generally nothing but a shed, per-

FIG. 32.

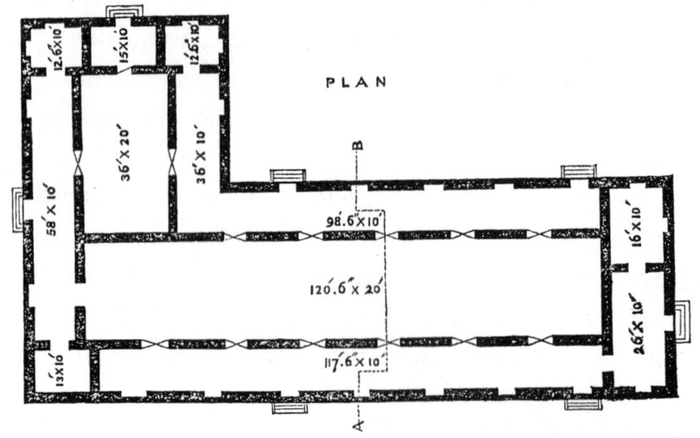

Plans, Sections, and Elevation of Native Hospital, Kurnool Fort.

Kurnool Fort Hospital.

Section on A B.

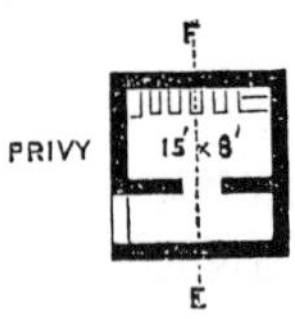

Section of Privy.

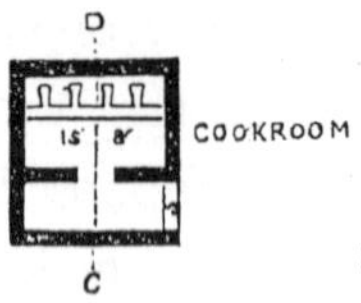

Section of Cook-room.

haps a "gun-shed," or a "cattle-shed," as at Kolapore, converted into a hospital, where the sick receive nothing but medicine. The patients cook their own diets, eating and drinking what they please. Or when too ill to cook for themselves, an orderly friend is detailed for the purpose. There are no conveniences; sometimes the sick go home to wash, or bathe themselves in a tank. Such are the "ward offices usually provided for these establishments." In one native infantry hospital at Secunderabad it is stated that hospital gangrene frequently occurs from overcrowding, from the cachectic state of the patients, *owing to the unhealthy character of their lines*, and from a cesspool in the hospital enclosure, which last is, however, being remedied.

At Rangoon, it is stated that the privies, for native regiments, are built of matting, "which is most objectionable, as allowing the escape of noxious effluvia." Is it then desired to keep the "noxious effluvia" *in?*

It is supposed that "caste" prejudices are such as to prevent native hospitals being properly built, and supplied with requisites for sick. But this has to be proved by giving natives a properly constructed and provided hospital. There are plenty of "caste prejudices" in this country against good hospital construction; but good hospital construction advances nevertheless.

At Loodiana, one native doctor, one cooly, one water-carrier, one sweeper, are the attendants "sufficient for the ordinary wants of the sick." The present arrangements for the female hospital are said to be "sufficient," (which means *none.*) (Loodiana is now a native station).

These native hospitals, again, combine all the disadvantages of civilization without any of its advantages. In one place the hospital was so overcrowded that for two years "gangrenous and spreading sores" were "frequent." In another it was so much out of repair that "it would before long be a ruin" (the best thing that could happen to it). If there is a privy it is a "small room, with no place in which the excrement can go to be cleared away." If there is a lavatory or bath, it is "two tubs out of repair," (does that mean that they cannot hold water?) If there is a kitchen, as at Mercara, it is under the same shed as a privy, and cannot be used for the stench. Indeed the medical officer proposes that it should be turned into a privy. The sick generally cook under the nearest tree, and if unable to do so, a comrade cooks for them under the tree. Linen is washed and dried by caste comrades, or by the patients when not too ill. Each patient brings in his own bedding; generally his own bedstead. "Each patient defers bathing, according to custom, till he is cured, when he retires to the nearest well, draws water, and undergoes the bath of cure," *i.e.*, when he no longer wants it. Every report begs for a bath-room.

These are the facts with regard to the constructive arrangements for sick and for administrative purposes in the various classes of Indian hospitals.

Some of the recent military hospitals are superior to those described. They are erected on what is called the standard plan, supposed to contain every necessary requirement, and issued for the guidance of local authorities.

Fig. 33 shows half of this plan. It consists of a large hut with sloping roof, supported by longitudinal and transverse arches, the latter of which divide it into six divisions, called wards, each of which is 48 feet long, 20 feet wide, and 18 feet high to the top of the wall. The building from end to end is intended for 96 beds, virtually in one long ward, at 1080 cubic feet, and 60 superficial feet per bed. The floor is raised 4 feet above the level of the ground; but there is no circulation of air beneath the floor.

There are six open fire-places in the closed verandah, which runs along one side of the hospital. The verandah on the other side is open. There is roof ventilation along the entire length. There is a non-commissioned officer's room at each end, with a door opening into the ward.

FIG. 33.

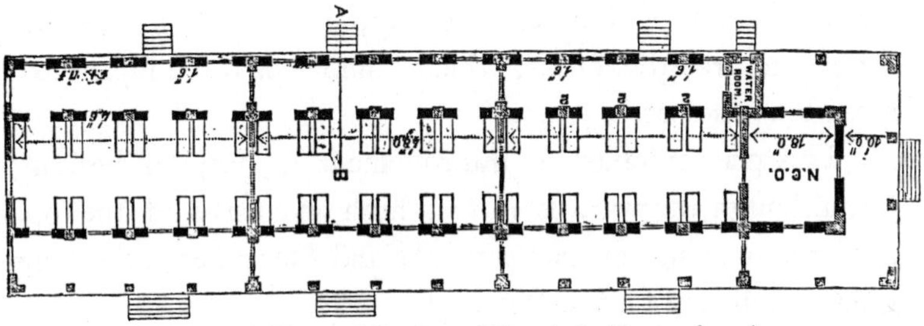

Standard Plan and Section of Hospital, Hazareebaugh.

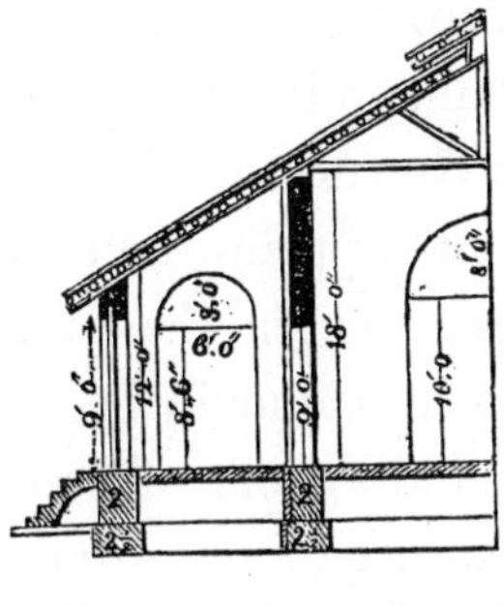

There are several favourable points in this construction, but it cannot by any means be taken as representing good hospital construction for a warm climate. There is no circulation of air beneath the floor; the hut forms, in reality, one long ward with 96 beds in it—just four times too many; and, as it is, the ventilation is obstructed by the transverse arches. The closed verandah along one side is inadmissible, if closed by anything else but jalousies,—except, indeed, in very exposed situations, subject to high winds. But even in such positions it is better to place the end of the building to the wind, and to leave the sides without closed verandahs, than it is to turn the side to the wind with closed verandahs.

The wall space per bed is smaller than I ever remember to have seen in any European hospital; pairs of beds appear to have only about 7 feet allotted to them. It is true there is a door or window between every two pairs of beds; but these, if used for ventilation, will necessarily expose the sick in the beds directly to draughts of air, which cannot fail to be injurious in not a few diseases.

This plan exhibits no improvement in hospital lighting; for, although the ward is 18 feet high, exclusive of the open roof, the openings in the verandahs and the arches in the longitudinal walls are only 9 feet high.

There are no ward offices; and the building can only be considered as an improved camp hospital.

It is very important to inquire on what general principles hospitals for Indian climates should hereafter be constructed. The defects in the present plans, taken in connexion with the local conditions described in the Reports, appear to indicate what these principles should be—*e.g.*, malaria is a constant product of the Indian soil. It rarely rises more than a few feet above the surface of the ground; but all who sleep within its sphere suffer more or less.

1. Out of this fact comes one great general principle—viz., that sick men in India should always sleep as high above the ground as the circumstances of the case admit of; the height will vary with locality. In high, well-drained positions, 4 or 5 feet will be enough; but in low, malarial districts, the sick should always be placed on upper floors. In every instance

there should be a free current of air between the ward floor and the ground.

2. In a warm climate it cannot be safe to agglomerate a large number of sick in one ward. It is unsafe in Europe. It cannot be less unsafe in India. What is wanted in a warm climate is a very free movement of the air around the sick, without exposing them to blasts or great variations of temperature. And all emanations from the sick should be discharged at once into the open air. To realize these advantages, the best method obviously is to subdivide the sick in separate detached buildings, containing, say, 24 beds each, or thereabouts, so arranged as to obtain the full benefit of prevailing healthy winds.

3. In all hospitals, but especially in hospitals in warm climates, the question as regards space is not simply one of cubic feet per bed; but it is mainly one of superficial area. What is wanted is a large body of comparatively pure air around each bed. The extent of area and space will of course differ according to the healthiness of the position. In high airy districts the surface area might approach to that of a cooler latitude, viz., 100 square feet, with 1500 cubic feet, which is now the regulation in Her Majesty's service for warm climate hospitals. In low, hot, moist, malarial localities, it would be better to have no hospitals. But as there must be sick, the space and area per bed should be increased in a corresponding degree, from 100 up to, say, 120 or 130 square feet, with from 1500 up to, say, 2000 cubic feet.

4. In a sick ward, simplicity of construction is essential to good ventilation. There should be no transverse arches or thick pillars, no double verandahs nor corridors. The ward should be perfectly open from end to end, and from side to side. The window space and door space should be

sufficient for light and ventilation. Dark hospitals are unfit for sick. It is not necessary for light and heat to go together.

The doors and windows should be on opposite sides. Verandahs are required for shelter from the sun. They should always be single and open, and of sufficient width to afford the requisite shade. Verandahs should never be constructed or used to supplement the sick accommodation, or for dining-rooms, or for convalescent day-rooms. All such accommodation should be provided at the end of the block and not along its sides.

5. In permanent hospitals the wards should be ceiled. They are more comfortable, cooler, and they look cleaner. The space between the ceiling and the roof should be freely ventilated to allow the hot air to escape. Double walls, where practicable, having a ventilating space between the outer and the inner wall, with openings above and below to allow a current of air to pass up, will always be cooler than any other construction, except the walls be very thick.

6. The question of wall space for beds is of great importance in hot climates. It is inadmissible to place a bed close beside an open door. Any arrangement of doors and windows which allows the wind to blow directly upon the sick should be avoided in future. There should be a space of at least three and a half feet between every two adjoining beds, if the beds are arranged in pairs. But it would be much better to construct wards which would allow the beds to stand at equal distances from each other. If each bed is allowed as a minimum 100 square feet of surface, and 1500 cubic feet, the bed might have from 8 to 10 linear feet of wall space. With wards 15 feet high, which is quite enough, an 8 feet wall space would enable the ward to be about 25 feet wide. A 10 feet

wall space would reduce the width to 20 feet, which is rather narrow for comfort.

When the larger amounts of cubic space and superficial area are given, the wall space per bed need not exceed 10 feet, and the additional surface should be thrown into the width of the ward, the height (15 feet) being retained.

As, in hot climates, all convalescents *must* be removed to convalescent wards, and as thus only serious cases, generally of fever or dysentery, will remain, the conclusion is, how doubly important a sufficient space and area!

7. Each ward should have its own ward offices. Or if two wards are placed in line, end to end, certain of the ward offices might be placed in the space between them outside the verandahs. These might be the ablution and bath-rooms, and scullery. The hospital sergeant's room must always be attached to and overlook one ward, if not both, and if not both, the orderly's room must overlook the other. Each ward should have a separate water-closet accessible from the verandah, but so arranged as to prevent the patient going out or holding communication with persons outside; and yet with a perfectly free cross ventilation between the closet and the ward.

8. Each ward, in such a climate as India, should have a bath with hot and cold water laid on. There should be a basin-stand with sunk basins and water laid on.

9. Were it not that there is not a hospital in India which is drained, it might appear quite superfluous to have to state that no building is fit for sick that is not thoroughly drained to an outlet.

10. Every hospital should have an abundant supply of pure water *laid on*, for all purposes. The present supply by water-carriers and bullocks is perfectly absurd.

11. Ventilation should always be ensured by a sufficient

number of louvred ventilating turrets carried straight from the ceiling of the ward through the roof. They should be so louvred as to prevent rain beating in, and they should be protected at the ceiling in such way as to prevent casual blasts of air in high winds from blowing upon the sick. Fresh air should always be admitted abundantly at the eaves. The fresh-air ventilator should be carried all the way round the hospital; there should be louvres to throw air-currents up towards the ceiling; the ventilation should be sufficient at ordinary times without doors or windows, but the doors and windows should be jalousied to be used for increasing the ventilation in still weather. The windows should always be glazed, which they are not at all invariably in India.

12. Each hospital kitchen should be supplied with improved cooking apparatus.

13. All the administrative offices should be in one block by themselves; the wards should only be for sick. If the hospital were on an upper floor, the administrative offices and stores might occupy the ground floor.

14. The medical and nursing attendants should never have to pass all their day upon the road, in going backwards and forwards, as is not at all unfrequently the case in India. Convenient quarters should be provided, and the regimental orderlies' rooms should be attached to their respective wards.

15. Each hospital should be provided with a covered ambulatory for convalescents.

16. Convalescent wards, and especially convalescent day and dining-rooms, are a necessity of all hot-climate military hospitals, more particularly during epidemics. Because a soldier must be in hospital or in barracks. To leave him, when recovering from fever or dysentery, among the fever and dysentery cases, or to make him return from a day-room to

sleep among them, is to consign him to an almost certain relapse. He should sleep in a convalescent ward, and eat and live in a convalescent day-room. But these convalescent wards must have a completely appointed nursing staff of their own, the same as sick wards have. Otherwise the convalescents will play tricks, and make themselves worse instead of better. And the day-room must be included in the supervision.

Convalescent accommodation will enable the hospital to be cleared much sooner than if convalescents are left to sleep, eat, and pass their time among men in all stages of the same epidemic malady from which they themselves may be recovering.

VIII.

HOSPITALS FOR SOLDIERS' WIVES AND CHILDREN.

Of late years a small number of hospitals for sick wives and children of soldiers have been erected in this country, on account of the very defective accommodation in married soldiers' quarters rendering due care of the sick, especially of cases of confinements, all but impossible. These new hospitals are constructed on the same plan as that adopted for regimental hospitals, figs. 21, 22. One half of the building is set apart for general cases, and the other for confinements. A small delivery ward is provided at one end of the long ward instead of the bath-room, which is not required; but in every other respect the plans are similar. Each hospital has a matron and such additional attendants as she may require. Wherever these hospitals have been provided, they have been of the greatest use.

There are female hospitals also in India, but they are constructed on a totally different plan. Some of them, as at Kurrachee and Deesa, Lucknow, Raneegunge and Ferozepore, appear to be very complete, with female attendants. In the Madras Presidency, they are too often, as at Bangalore, Trichinopoly, and Kamptee, merely men's wards appropriated to women, and justly stated to be "objectionable in every way." Elsewhere they are rather bare. Indeed, as at Baroda, Kirkee, Poona, Darjeeling, the sick women and children " have to be attended at their own quarters," either because " there is no matron," or because the " ward is too small," or, &c. &c. Curiously enough, it is generally stated that the " present arrangement is conducive to comfort." What arrangement? Of having no matron? While it is added, that a lying-in ward and a matron are " much wanted." At Darjeeling the women and children are treated in their own quarters, which " would be satisfactory enough if the married quarters were not so dark and damp as they are." Sometimes it is said that " the arrangements are quite equal to those for the men."

The construction of these hospitals appears to be the same as that of small regimental hospitals.

The following plan and section of a female hospital at Meean Meer (one of the most recently built in India) shows that they require quite as much structural improvement. It is a nest of rooms within rooms; and the same may be said of it

FIG. 34.

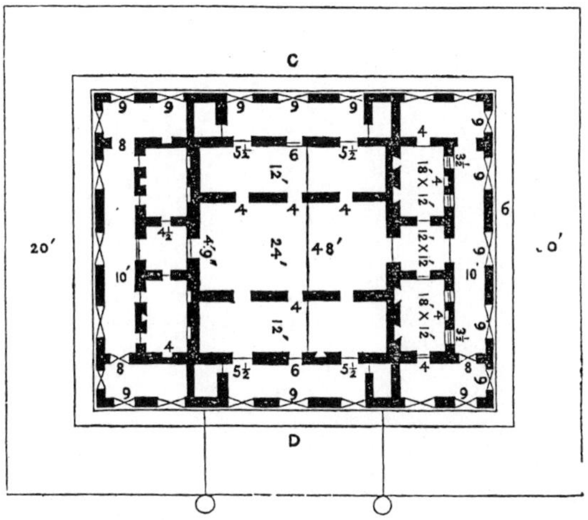

Plan and Section of Female Hospital, Meean Meer.

that one of our engineers said of the Pacha's new fort on the Dardanelles, that "he would be much safer outside of it."

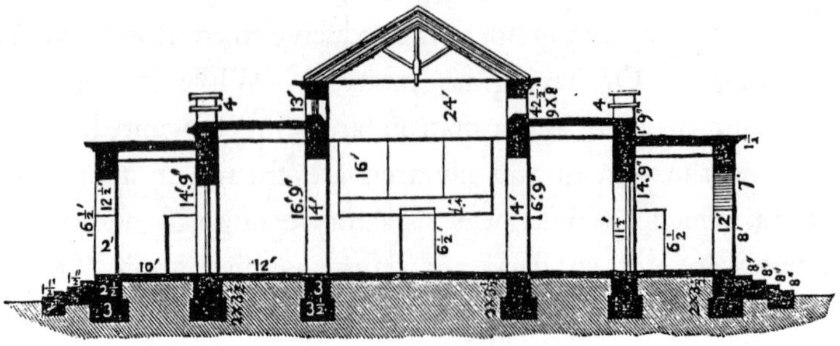

Section on C D.

IX.

HOSPITAL STATISTICS.

In the first edition of my Notes on Hospitals the defects of existing systems of hospital statistics were pointed out, and it was proposed to collect and tabulate certain elements for each hospital on one uniform plan. This plan was laid before the London meeting of the International Statistical Congress, and was adopted by the Congress with a few additions. The special question of statistics of surgical operations had subsequently to be considered. In the present section will be given the substance of my former communications, as well as the new proposal for tabulating all operations on one uniform plan.

These methods, if generally used, would enable us to ascertain the mortality in different hospitals, as well as from different diseases and injuries at the same and at different ages, the relative frequency of different diseases and injuries among the classes which enter hospitals in different countries, and in different districts of the same country. They would enable us to ascertain how much of each year of life is wasted by illness,—what diseases and ages press most heavily on the resources of particular hospitals. For example, it was found that a very large proportion of the limited finances of one hospital was swallowed up by one preventible disease,—Rheumatism,—to the exclusion of many important cases or other diseases from the benefits of the hospital treatment.

The relation of the duration of cases to the general utility of a hospital requires also to be shown, because it must be obvious that if, by any sanitary means or improved treatment, the duration of cases could be reduced to one-half, the utility of the hospital would be doubled, so far as its funds are concerned.

This section is divided into two heads, the first referring to the general method laid before the Congress; the second, to an additional proposal for a uniform method of recording the results of surgical operations.

A. General Statistics of Hospitals.

In the appended Table for registering Hospital Statistics, the nomenclature agreed to at the Paris meeting of the Statistical Congress has been adopted, with two or three slight modifications, referring chiefly to rare diseases; and the proposed classification is essentially the same as that used by the Registrars-General of the United Kingdom.

The form itself has been in use for many years in the Registrar-General's office, for the registration of deaths; and has hence the advantage of having been fully tried by experience. Each Table is divided vertically into columns containing the ages in monthly and yearly periods from under 1 year to 5. Above 5 the ages are given quinquennially.

The disease list is divided into two sections, one printed on the left hand, the other on the right of the sheet. The left-hand division contains the diseases more frequently admitted into hospital; the right-hand the rarer forms of disease.

This arrangement is necessary for the purpose of limiting the size of the Tables.

Worms . . .
OTHERS . . . .

CLASS II.—ORDER I.
(CONSTITUTIONAL DISEASES.)

Gout
Dropsy
Cancer
Canker (noma)
Mortification
OTHERS

ORDER II.

Scrofula
Tuberculosis Mesenterica
Phthisis
Hæmoptysis
Pneumothorax
Hydrocephalus (with tubercular deposit)
OTHERS

CLASS III.—ORDER I.
(LOCAL DISEASES.)

A. Brain, spinal marrow, and nerves.

Meningitis
Cephalitis (including acute hydrocephalus)
Paralysis
Chorea
Mania
Epilepsy
Hysteria
Tetanus (idiopathic)
Convulsions
OTHERS

B. Sense organs.

Ophthalmitis (not purulent)
Cataract
Amaurosis
Glaucoma and other diseases of the eye
Otorrhœa
Otitis
Deafness and other diseases of the ear
OTHERS

ORDER II.

Carditis
Pericarditis
Endocarditis
Disease of Heart Valves
Heart Hypertrophy
,, Atrophy
,, Fatty degeneration
Aneurism of heart
Aneurism of aorta, &c.
Angina Pectoris
Fainting
Phlebitis
Varix
OTHERS

ORDER III.

Epistaxis
Laryngitis (Œdema of the glottis)
Bronchitis
Pleurisy
Pneumonia
Asthma
OTHERS

ORDER IV.

Gastritis
Enteritis
Peritonitis
Constipation
Colic
Ileus (Obstruction of bowels)
Intussusception
Hernia
Stricture of œsophagus
Stricture of intestinal tube
Ulceration of intestinal tube
Dyspepsia
Pyrosis
Gastralgia
Hæmatemesis
Apoplexy
Melæna
Hæmorrhoids
Fistula
Pancreatic disease
Spleen disease
Hepatitis
Jaundice
Gall Stones
Cirrhosis
Ascites
OTHERS

ORDER V.

Nephritis
Ischuria
Nephria (Bright's disease, Albuminuria)
Diabetes
Stone (uric Acid, &c.)
Gravel (uric Acid, &c.
Hæmaturia
Cystitis
Disease of Prostate Gland
OTHERS

ORDER VI.

Varicocele
Hydrocele
Ovarian Dropsy
OTHERS

ORDER VII.

Synovitis
Ostitis (including periostitis and endostitis)
Exostosis
Curvature of Spine
Caries
Necrosis
Muscular Atrophy
OTHERS

ORDER VIII.

Phlegmon
Whitlow
Abscess (external)
Ulcer (external)
OTHER SKIN diseases

CLASS IV.—ORDER I.
(DEVELOPMENTAL DISEASES.)

Spina bifida
OTHER malformations
Teething
OTHERS

ORDER II.

Chlorosis
Childbirth { Miscarriage / Abortion, &c.
Paramenia (including Amenorrhœa, Leucorrhœa, Turn of Life, Climacteria)

CLASS V.—VIOLENT DEATHS OR DISEASES.

ORDER I.—(ACCIDENT.)

Burn
Scald
Fracture
Contusion
Concussion
Gunshot wound
Cut, stab
Poisoning
OTHERS

ORDER III.—(HOMICIDE.)
ORDER IV.—(SUICIDE.)

Gunshot wound
Cut, stab
Poisoning
OTHERS

Sudden deaths (cause not ascertained)
Causes not specified or ill-defined

TOTAL . . .

---

malignant pustule
necusia*
* *Infection by puncture in dissection or by handling the parts of dead animals.*

ORDER III.

rickets
bronchocele
cretinism
ergotism

ORDER IV.

phthiriasis
Hydatids, tape worm, and other entozoa should be distinguished here. In the capital table they will be added to the head "Worms."

CLASS II.

ORDER I.

anæmia
lupus
dry gangrene
bed sore
melanosis
The several forms of cancer comprised in the capital table under the head "Cancer" should be distinguished as under; the ages, and parts affected, should also be specified:
Soft
Colloid
Osteoid
Scirrhus
Epithelial

ORDER II.

psoas abscess
scrofulous abscess of joints (placed to *scrofula*)
tubercular peritonitis

CLASS III.

ORDER I.

myelitis
shaking palsy (placed to *paralysis*)
The parts affected, in all cases referred to "paralysis" in the capital table, should be distinguished here, and the ages stated.
monomania (placed to *mania*)
dementia (placed to *mania*)
laryngismus stridulus
The different parts of the eye attacked by inflammation should be distinguished here.
neuralgia (tic douloureux)
neuroma

ORDER II.

arteritis
atheroma (of arteries)

ORDER III.

hydrothorax
empyema
pleuripneumonia (placed to *pneumonia*)
congestion of lungs (placed to *pneumonia*)
emphysema (of lungs)
spurious melanosis

ORDER IV.

glossitis
stomatitis
pharyngitis
æsophagitis
Distinguish here the following varieties of hernia, all of which are classed in the capital table under hernia:
congenital
femoral or *crural*
inguinal
scrotal
umbilical
ventral

ORDER V.

diuresis
stricture of urethra (not a consequence of gonorrhœa)
In cases of stone and gravel, the composition of substances should be specified here.

ORDER VI.

orchitis
hysteritis
ovarian tumour
uterine tumour
polypus of uterus

ORDER VII.

fragilitas ossium
mollities ossium

ORDER VIII.

roseola
urticaria
eczema
herpes
pemphigus
ecthyma
impetigo
acne
mentagra
lichen
prurigo
psoriasis
pityriasis
ichthyosis
In abscess and ulcer the parts affected should be distinguished here.

CLASS IV.

malformations
anus imperforatus
cyanosis
decay of old age
atrophy and debility

CLASS V.

ORDER I.

explosion of powder, gas, &c. (placed to *burn*)
chilblains
frost-bite
lightning, (where struck and how?)
sun-stroke (state circumstances)
The circumstances attending deaths by violence should be shown in detail; as, for example, how many persons, at their several ages, were burnt by their clothes taking fire, how many died by falling from scaffolds or heights, how many were poisoned by arsenic, opium, quack medicine, over-dose, &c. Gunshot wounds should be distinguished as regards the species of weapon,—rifle, pistol, cannon, &c.; other wounds, as whether inflicted by knife, dagger, &c. When cases of privation, drowning, hanging, suffocation, fall within observation, they should be placed to "Others" in the general Table, and the particulars should be stated here. All violent deaths should fall under one or other of the three orders: Accident—Homicide—Suicide.

[*To face p.* 160]

In allotting the diseases between these two columns, advantage has been taken of the experience gained in filling up the forms by different hospitals.

The facts in regard to the diseases in the left-hand column, being those of most frequent occurrence in hospitals, are to be entered directly in the columns of the Table. The name of any disease not found in the left-hand column is to be looked for in the right-hand one, and the ages of the persons affected are to be placed after the name. The *class* and *order* in which the case stands is then to be sought for in the left-hand column, and a mark or marks, as the case may be, are to be placed in the "age" column in the line "others." Should any very rare case present itself, not included in the right-hand column, it should be written-in under its proper class and order, and entered in the left-hand column under the head "others" as before.

These exceptional cases will only afford statistical results of value after periods of years; and they should be extracted separately.

It is proposed that one and the same form should be used for each statistical element. Seven elements are required to enable us to tabulate the results of hospital experience; they are as follow:—

1. Remaining in hospital on the first day of the year.
2. Admitted during the year.
3. Recovered or relieved during the year.
4. Discharged incurable, unrelieved, for irregularities, or at their own request.
5. Died during the year.
6. Remaining in hospital on the last day of the year.
7. Mean duration of cases in days and fractions of a day.

These seven elements printed as separate headings and

attached to copies of the same form, or written-in, would furnish us with the means of tabulating every fact we require. Provision can be made for different sexes in one of two ways: the column for each age may be subdivided for males and females; or it might be more convenient to have two sets of forms, one for each sex.

Again, surgical cases and injuries may be included in the same form with medical cases; or, in large hospitals, a separate set of forms might be devoted to surgical cases.

For small hospitals, one set of seven forms might easily be made to contain the annual statistics of ages, sexes, and diseases (medical and surgical); but for very large hospitals, possibly four sets might be required.

The primary object of these Tables is to obtain an uniform record of facts from which to deduce statistical results, among which the following may be mentioned:—

1. The total *sick population—i.e.*, the number of beds constantly occupied during the year by each disease for each age and sex.
2. The *number of cases* of each age, sex, and disease submitted to (medical or surgical) treatment during the year.
3. The *average duration* in days and parts of a day of each disease for each sex and age.
4. The *mortality* from each disease for each sex and age.
5. The annual proportion of *recoveries* to beds occupied and to cases treated for each age, sex, and disease.

In reducing the data to give the annual results, either percentages or per-thousands may be used.

The number of beds constantly occupied may be obtained by taking the mean of the numbers remaining at the beginning and end of the year, if the hospital has been fully occupied; or the mean of the numbers remaining at the beginning and end of each quarter; or oftener, if the hospital be irregularly occupied; or, the total number of days spent in hospital by all the cases during the year might be obtained; and by dividing the sum by 365, the mean daily sick would be arrived at. [The total daily "*diets*" issued during the year divided by 365 would give the same result.]

The "*sick treated*" during the year may be obtained by taking the mean of the admissions, and of the discharges from all causes, including deaths.

With fixed data, arrived at on these principles, we can readily obtain the proportionate mortality, not only of the whole hospital, but of every ward of it, and also the proportionate mortality and duration of cases for each age, sex, and disease.

It need hardly be pointed out of what great practical value these and similar results would become, if obtained over a large number of hospitals.

The laws which regulate diseased action would become better known, the results of particular methods of treatment, as well as of special operations, would be better ascertained than they are at present. As regards their sanitary condition, hospitals might be compared with hospitals and wards with wards.

The whole question of hospital economics as influenced by diets, medicines, comforts, could be brought under examination and discussion.

The liability of particular ages, sexes, occupations, and classes of the community to particular forms of disease might be ascertained; other data, such as "married" or "single," previous attacks of illness of the same or of different kinds, birthplace, &c., might be added for comparison, and hospital

M 2

experience might thus be made to subserve sanitary improvement.

The data for these latter comparisons would have to be kept separately, as indeed they generally are in all well-regulated hospitals.

The present proposal for improved hospital statistics is confined to those points bearing directly on the welfare of sick admitted to the wards.

The work has been materially assisted by the kindness of the authorities of St. Thomas's, University College, and St. Mary's Hospitals, who have been at great pains in having the experimental sheets (sent to them) accurately filled up, and to whom grateful acknowledgments are here expressed.

These forms are now in use in St. Bartholomew's Hospital and in London Hospital; and the recommendations of the Statistical Congress have led to a greater uniformity in keeping the records of several other large hospitals.

The forms are intended solely for the tabulation of cases, whether of in-patients or out-patients, but the Congress considered it to be advisable that certain other data should be recorded; and it made the following recommendations, in which I cordially agree.

1. The publication in the Annual Report of a TABULAR STATEMENT, not only of the total number of patients, but also of the total number of *cases of disease*, under the various heads, distinguishing the diseases which have supervened in the hospital.
2. That in the *registration of cases*, not only the disease for which the patient is admitted, but also those by which he is subsequently affected, be separately recorded.

3. That not only the date of admission into hospital, but the date of attack be recorded.
4. That the date of admission be noted, so as to be compared with the disease, occupation, and age of the patients.
5. That in transferring patients from medical to surgical wards, or *vice versâ*, an uniform method of record be adopted.
6. That the exact locality in which the disease originated should, as far as possible, be recorded.
7. That a system of registration of *out*-patients at hospitals and dispensaries be adopted on a similar classification (as far as practicable) to that of the in-patients.
8. That in hospital statistics the average proportion of empty beds be noted, both for the whole year, and also for the different seasons.
9. That the average cost of each *in*- and *out*-patient be noted under the different heads of (*a*) food, &c., (*b*) officers and nurses, (*c*) drugs, &c., (*d*) sundries.
10. That in all hospitals supported by private subscriptions, both the number of *in*- and *out*-patients be noted, and also the number of letters of recommendation given.
11. That previous diseases of patients, and diseases and habits of parents, be (as far as possible) noted.
12. That in hospitals there be tabulated :—

    The number of beds.
    The number of storeys.
    The number of wards.
    The length, breadth, and height of wards.
    The number of beds per ward.

The cubic feet per bed.
The superficial area per bed.
Number of windows, with their dimensions.
Means of ventilation.
Drainage.
Water-closets or latrines.
Water supply.

THE following heads for a Hospital Admission and Discharge Book will afford a ready means of collecting the data required for filling up the annual forms proposed in this section. They also include those particulars in regard to cases of disease contained in the additional propositions adopted by the Congress.

HOSPITAL ADMISSION AND DISCHARGE BOOK.

No. of Case.	Date of Admission.	Name.	Age.	Sex, M. or F.	Residence, and Place where taken ill, or Injured.	Trade or Occupation.	Disease or Accident.	Date.					Duration of Case in Hospital in Days and Quarters.	Remarks. — (Previous Diseases of Patients and of Parents.)
								Of Attack.	Of Recovery.	Of Death.	Of Discharge, (Relieved) or (unrelieved), or otherwise.	Of Transfer to other Division of Hospital.		

NOTE.—If a patient admitted for one disease (such as ulcer) is attacked by another disease (such as erysipelas), unconnected with the former, the patient *should not be "discharged."* The new disease should simply be entered as *another case*, and the date of recovery from the first disease (ulcer) should not be filled up until the ulcer is healed. At the same time as the entry of the new disease (erysipelas) is made, a note should be written in the discharge column of the admission for ulcer, simply referring to the new number under which the case is entered, thus (See No.). The date of recovery, death, &c., from the second disease, erysipelas, must be entered in the proper column opposite that disease.

The following Annual Tabular Abstracts for the Yearly Report of the Hospital embody the other recommendations of the Congress :—

I. In-Patients.

Periods.	No. of Letters of Recommendation.*		Admissions.		Total Cases of Disease treated.†		Deaths.		Recoveries.		Otherwise discharged.		No. of Beds occupied.					
													Maximum.		Minimum.		Average.	
	M.	F.	M.	F.	M.	F.	M.	F.	M.	F.	M.	F.	M.	F.	M.	F.	M.	F.
1st Quarter . . .																		
2nd Quarter . . .																		
3rd Quarter . . .																		
4th Quarter . . .																		
Total for the Year .																		

* These columns are only required for Hospitals for which Letters of Recommendation are necessary.

† This column includes cases of disease occurring in patients *after* admission to Hospital.

2. Out-Patients.

Periods.	No. of Letters of Recommendation.*		No. of Patients.	
	Males.	Females.	Males.	Females.
1st Quarter				
2nd Quarter				
3rd Quarter				
4th Quarter				
Total for the Year .				

* These columns are only required for Hospitals for which Letters of Recommendation are necessary.

3. Cost of each Patient.

—	Food, &c., Wine, Spirits, Malt Liquor.	Officers and Nurses.	Drugs, &c. Instruments.	Other Expenses.			Total.
				Washing.	Firing and Lighting.	Sundries.	
In-Patients . . .							
Out-Patients . . .							

4.—Sanitary Statistics of Wards.

Number of Wards.	No. of Beds per Ward.	Dimensions of Wards.			Cubic Feet per Bed.	Superficial Feet per Bed.	Windows.			No. of Fire-places.	Ventilation if by (Windows) or (Ventilators), and its Sufficiency by Day and Night.	Number of		
		Length.	Breadth	Height.			Number.	Height.	Width.			Water-closets.	Baths.	Ablution Basins.
Ground Floor.														
No. 1.														
No. 2, &c.														
First Floor.														
No. 1.														
No. 2, &c.														
Second Floor.														
No. 1.														
No. 2, &c.														

State of Drainage - { Good. / Indifferent. / Bad. / Cesspits, &c.

State of Water-Supply. - { Quality - { Good. / Indifferent. / Bad. ; Quantity - { Sufficient. / Insufficient.

B. Proposal for Improved Statistics of Surgical Operations.

Some time ago the attention of the medical profession was occupied with an important discussion on the mortality from surgical operations, resulting in certain conclusions as to the causes of this mortality in different hospitals and in different countries.

Having been engaged some time previously in endeavouring to further a more uniform system of hospital statistics generally than had previously existed, I was naturally interested in the discussions alluded to, and a very cursory examination of the statistical data adduced was sufficient to satisfy any one that the real mortality due to operations had not as yet been ascertained with sufficient accuracy to enable a just comparison to be made. The data employed may be described as follows:—

So many operations of such and such a nature, without reference to age, sex, or cause of the operation, followed by so many deaths, without reference to age, sex, or complications.

Given these elements, divide the one by the other, and you get the mortality.

A statistical proceeding such as this can at best lead to very loose approximations. It can convey but a very imperfect idea of the real state of the case. And one thing is quite certain, that it can lead to no practical result whatever, either as regards the true causes of the mortality, or how these may be mitigated.

The first step in the way of improvement is to obtain a terse and accurate registration of the elements of the problem. Every well-kept hospital record ought to contain these. But for the sake of uniformity, I enumerate them as follows:—

1. Age.
2. Sex.
3. Occupation.
4. Accident or disease leading to operation.
5. Date of accident and of operation, or date of operation if from disease.
6. Nature of operation.
7. Constitution of patient.
8. Complications occurring after operation.
9. Date of recovery or of death.
10. Fatal complication. *a.* Resulting directly from the accident. *b.* Occurring after the operation.

These elements are of so much importance, that it would be well to enter them in a separate operation-book.

Having obtained them, the next step is to tabulate them for use; and to do this properly two forms are required.

1. Including all the operations, with their results.
2. For registering fatal cases.

Copies of these forms are appended.

Table I. is for tabulating the surgical operations performed. In this table, the ordinary English nomenclature of operations is adopted (with its numerous Anglicized Latin and Greek words) as the one most generally in use. The great operations are classed under two separate heads—those resulting from injury; those rendered necessary by disease. By so doing, we are able to eliminate the effect of shock, and also of the state of health of the patient; the former consequent on the accident, the latter as influencing the result of the operation.

After several trials, the sexes and the ages have been given for quinquennial periods up to 20 years, thence to 60 by decennial periods, and from 60 onwards again, by quin-

....

.... to ....

TABLE I.—SURGICAL OPERATIONS PERFORMED.

AGE AND SEX.																								RESULTS.				DISEASES OR INJURIES REQUIRING OPERATION.	COMPLICATIONS OCCURRING AFTER OPERATION. [After each complication, give the age of the patient.]	Average Duration in Days from Operation to Result.†	Remarks on Constitution of Patient, &c.
5—		10—		15—		20—		30—		40—		50—		60—		65—		70—		75 and above.		TOTAL.		Recovered.		Died.					
Males.	Females.	Males.	Females.	Males.	Females.	Males.	Females.	Males.	Females.	Males.	Females.	Males.	Females.	Males.	Females.	Males.	Females.	Males.	Females.	Males.	Females.	Males.	Females.	Males.	Females.	Males.	Females.				

...ded amputations through the joint next above, *e.g.*, under amputations of the leg those through knee-joint, unless where the amputation at the joint is expressly named.

† As a general rule, the result should be considered as attained at the date of the healing of the operation wound.

[*To face p.* 172].

....

.... to ....

.)

TABLE II.—MORTALITY FROM SURGICAL OPERATIONS.

AGE AND SEX.																								DISEASES OR INJURIES REQUIRING OPERATION.	FATAL COMPLICATION AND CAUSE OF DEATH. [After each complication give the age of the patient.]	Average Duration in Days from Operation till Death.		Remarks on Constitution of Patient, &c.
5 —		10 —		15 —		20 —		30 —		40 —		50 —		60 —		65 —		70 —		75 —		TOTAL DEATHS.						
Males.	Females.	Males.	Females.	Males.	Females.	Males.	Females.	Males.	Females.	Males.	Females.	Males.	Females.	Males.	Females.	Males.	Females.	Males.	Females.	Males.	Females.	Males.	Females.			Males.	Females.	

* Under amputations through any part of the limb should be included amputations through the joint next above, *e.g.*, under amputations of the leg those through knee joint, unless where the amputation at the joint is expressly named.

[*To face p.* 173].

quennial periods. This enables the influence of each (sex and age) on the result of operations to be ascertained. For the purposes of abstracting, the disease or injury requiring operation should in every instance be tabulated in a word or two. A column has therefore been provided for this purpose.

The most important perhaps of all the elements are the complications occurring after operation. It is these which mainly determine the result of the case, while they at the same time afford the most insight into preventible causes of mortality. As it is a matter of primary importance to adopt a common nomenclature of complications, one has been prepared, which is printed on each form for reference.

In filling up the column of complications, this nomenclature should be as far as possible adopted. It has been tried on an experience of upwards of 800 operations, in 141 of which there were distinct complications. The first result of the tabulation was to show that 66 of these complications were referable to pyæmia, cellular inflammation, erysipelas, sloughing, suppuration, gangrene, diarrhœa, and bedsore, diseases notoriously connected with defective sanitary conditions in wards, or with constitutions in patients so bad as to render doubtful the propriety of operating at all.

Table No. II. is intended to tabulate the fatal complications and causes of death. It is constructed to correspond with Table No. I., in order that, by simple arithmetical processes, the mortality from each operation for each sex and age, and also for each complication, may be readily ascertained. The same nomenclature, both of operations and of complications, is adopted in this as in the other Table; and two columns are added in which to enter the average duration of the cases (in days) from the date of the operation to that of the death.

The causes of death in 482 fatal operations have been

compared in this way: and one result has been to discover that 190 deaths (or nearly 40 per cent. of the total mortality) were occasioned by pyæmia, phlebitis, cellular inflammation, erysipelas, sloughing, suppuration, gangrene, diphtheria, pneumonia, and fevers, typhoid and hectic. No less than 50 deaths occurred from these two last diseases. Another result has been to ascertain the great difference in relative frequency of complications in different hospitals.

Thus out of three large hospitals, one returns 25 per cent. of its mortality after operations as being due to the fevers mentioned above; while the other two hospitals return not a single death from fever. In one of the hospitals, 27 per cent. of the deaths are returned as due to shock; in another 2½ per cent.; in another less than 1 per cent. are attributed to this cause. In one hospital 33 per cent. of the deaths are attributed to peritonitis; in another 3½ per cent., and in the third 22 per cent. The deaths from pyæmia are returned from one hospital as amounting to 12 per cent. of the total mortality; from another at 4½ per cent., and from a third at 14 per cent. Cellular inflammation, erysipelas, sloughing, suppuration, and gangrene, together yield in one hospital a proportion of 2 per cent.; in another 6 per cent.; in another 15 per cent. of the total mortality.

The comparative frequency of complications, not attended by fatal results, varies in an equal degree. The facts already ascertained, imperfect as they are, point to the following consequences:—First: That the sanitary condition of the hospitals has a much greater effect on the result of operations than could have been anticipated. Second: That in describing the complications, the same name is not always used to signify the same thing. The data at my disposal are too limited to allow of the comparative effect of age and sex on mortality being discovered; but, incomplete as they are, they all go to prove the necessity for adopting a uniform nomenclature of complications, and a uniform method of tabulation.

The one drawn up will, I believe, be found suitable for every purpose: it has been tried on a somewhat large scale and has been found to answer.

Every annual hospital report should contain a digest of the previous and past years' statistics, including those of its operations, on a uniform plan. For the general registration of cases, the forms and method given above, which were submitted to the Statistical Congress, and laid before the meeting of the Social Science Association at Dublin, will be found to answer the purpose; and the forms for registering operations I now submit, complete the work I took in hand.

It will not, of course, be necessary to print the entire forms in each annual report. In most hospitals not above a dozen or fifteen lines will be required every year. In the trials I have made, I find that the complications following on 811 operations can all be included in thirty-four lines, and this is a much larger number of operations than is ever likely to be registered in any one year in any hospital. In the smaller class of country hospitals the annual Table would rarely exceed half-a-dozen lines, so that no one need be alarmed at the apparent magnitude of the Tables.

I am fain to sum up with an urgent appeal for adopting this or some *uniform* system of publishing the statistical records of hospitals. There is a growing conviction that in all hospitals, even in those which are best conducted, there is a great and unnecessary waste of life; and that, as a general rule, the poor would recover better in their own miserable dwellings if they had proper medical and surgical aid, and efficient nursing, than they do under more refined treatment in hospitals. But few have had so sad or so large an experience as I have had to lead them to this conviction. It is imperative that this impression should be either dissipated or confirmed.

In attempting to arrive at the truth, I have applied everywhere for information, but in scarcely an instance have I been able to obtain hospital records fit for any purposes of comparison. If they could be obtained, they would enable us to decide many other questions besides the one alluded to. They would show subscribers how their money was being spent, what amount of good was really being done with it, or whether the money was not doing mischief rather than good: they would tell us the exact sanitary state of every hospital and of every ward in it, where to seek for causes of insalubrity and their nature; and, if wisely used, these improved statistics would tell us more of the relative value of particular operations and modes of treatment than we have any means of ascertaining at present. They would enable us, besides, to ascertain the influence of the hospital with its numerous diseased inmates, its overcrowded and possibly ill-ventilated wards, its bad site, bad drainage, impure water, and want of cleanliness—or the reverse of all these—upon the general course of operations and diseases passing through its wards; and the truth thus ascertained would enable us to save life and suffering, and to improve the treatment and management of the sick and maimed poor.

NOMENCLATURE OF OPERATIONS INTENDED TO BE USED IN FILLING UP TABLES I. AND II.

(*The operations should, for the sake of uniformity, be inserted in the Table in the order in which they stand in this list.*)

AMPUTATIONS (FOR INJURY) :—

Primary :—

Hip joint.
Thigh.
Leg.
Foot.
Toes.
Shoulder joint.
Arm.
Fore-arm.
Hand.
Fingers.

Secondary :—

Hip joint.
Thigh.
Leg.
Foot.
Toes.
Shoulder joint.
Arm.
Fore-arm.
Hand.
Fingers.

AMPUTATIONS (FOR DISEASE) :—

Hip joint.
Thigh.
Leg.
Ankle joint.
Foot.
Toes.
Shoulder joint.
Arm.
Fore-arm.
Hand.
Fingers.

HERNIA.

Inguinal :—Radical Cure.
Herniotomy—Opening Sac.
Without opening.
Femoral :—Radical Cure.
Herniotomy—Opening Sac.
Without opening.
Umbilical Hernia :—Opening Sac.
Without opening.

LITHOTOMY.

LITHOTRITY.

Urethrotomy :—For Calculus.
For Stricture.

EXCISION AND REMOVAL OF TUMOURS.

Cancer of Breast.
Other Tumours of Breast.
(State nature.)
Cancer of Lip.
Encysted of Scalp.
Glandular.
(State nature.)
Exostosis.
Other Tumours, Cancerous or Recurrent.
(State nature.)
Not Cancerous.
(State nature.)
Polypi :—Nasal.

Uterine.
Others.
(State nature.)

EXCISION (including TREPHINING) OF BONES AND JOINTS.

For Disease :—

Humerus.
Ditto, Head of.
Clavicle.
Scapula.
Elbow joint.
Ulna.
Radius.
Carpus.
Metacarpus.
Fingers.
Hip joint.
Pelvis.
Femur.
Knee joint.
Tibia.
Fibula.
Ankle joint.
Tarsus.
Metatarsus.
Toes.
Cranium.
Jaw, upper.
Ditto, lower
Vertebra.

For Injury :—

Humerus.
Ditto, Head of.
Clavicle.
Scapula.
Elbow joint.
Ulna.
Radius.
Carpus.
Metacarpus.
Fingers.
Hip joint.
Pelvis.
Femur.
Knee joint.
Tibia.
Fibula.
Ankle joint.
Tarsus.
Metatarsus.
Toes.
Cranium.
Jaw, upper.
Ditto, lower.
Vertebra.

Removal of Sequestra: — From Head.
From Trunk.
,, Upper Extremities.
,, Lower Extremities.

TRACHEOTOMY.

LARYNGOTOMY.

ŒSOPHAGOTOMY.

ABDOMINAL SECTION : — Ovariotomy.
Gastrotomy.
Opening of Colon.
Cæsarean Section.

REPARATORY OPERATIONS.

Cicatrices and Contractions (from Burns and other Injuries.)
Deformities from Disease.
,, ,, Injuries.

Deformities Congenital :—Hare Lip.
Others.
Cleft or Defective Palate.

PARACENTESIS.

Abdominal.
Hydrocele.
Ovarian.
Thoracic.
Vesical.
Cephalic.
Spinal.

EVACUATION OF CYSTS AND TUMOURS.

SECTIONS OF SOFT PARTS.

Perineal Section.

Fistula.

Anal and Rectal Ulcers.

Hæmorrhoids.

Partial Excision of Organs.

Extraction of Loose Cartilages.

„ Balls and other Foreign Bodies.

Internal Division of Stricture :—

Urethra.

Of Rectum.

Others.

TENOTOMY.

MYOTOMY.

REMOVAL OF PARTS BY LIGATURE.

Nævi.

Hæmorrhoids.

Tongue.

Others.

REMOVAL OF PARTS BY ECRASEUR.

LIGATURE OF ARTERIES.

For Aneurism.
(State nature.)

For Hæmorrhage.

For other Diseases and Injuries.
(State nature.)

OBLITERATION OF VEINS.

OPHTHALMIC OPERATIONS.

Extraction.

Dislocation.

Keratonyxis.

Artificial Pupil.

Strabismus.

Excision of Eye.

NOMENCLATURE OF COMPLICATIONS OCCURRING AFTER OPERATIONS.

The same nomenclature is to be used in filling up the column of FATAL *complications in Table II.*

[In filling up the column of complications in Tables I. and II., it is proposed, for the sake of uniformity, that the following nomenclature of the more common complications be adopted] :—

Shock.

Accidents from chloroform or other anæsthetics.

Exhaustion, from accident.

„ „ operation.

Delirium tremens.

„ traumatic :

Tetanus.

Coma.

Hæmorrhage, continuous.

„ recurring.

„ secondary (state in a note the times of its recurrence).

Acute inflammation, in or near the seat of operation, such as—

Peritonitis.

„ hernial.

Pleuritis.

Pyelitis.

Cystitis.

Pneumonia.

Of Brain or Membranes.

(Distinguishing such as are the direct result of the wound in operation by adding the word "traumatic.")

Necrosis.
Fistula.
Pyæmia, acute.
„ chronic.
(Including
Purulent infection,
Purulent diathesis,
Putrid infection.)
Pyæmial pneumonia.
Gangrene:—
Primary.
Secondary.
Hospital.
Diphtheria of wounds.
Phagedæna.
Sloughing.
„ of intestine (hernial).
Erysipelas, simple.
„ phlegmonous.
Cellular inflammation (including purulent œdema, sloughing, and suppuration of cellular tissue).
Extravasation of urine.
Phlebitis.
Inflamed lymphatics.
Fevers, typhus.
„ „ hospital.
„ typhoid.
„ hectic.
„ scarlet.
Measles.
Diarrhœa.
Tuberculosis, phthisis, &c.
Scurvy.
Diphtheria.
Bed-sore.
Vomiting.
Cancerous cachexia.
Continuance of disease.
Recurrence of „
Croup.
„ (after tracheotomy).
Internal strangulation (hernial).
Secondary diseases of liver.
„ „ heart.
„ „ kidney, &c.

[Any other complication, not included in this list, may be inserted under its usual name.]

APPENDIX.

ON DIFFERENT SYSTEMS OF HOSPITAL NURSING.

In the important question of accommodation for nurses, so much depends upon the method of nursing chosen, that an Appendix is devoted to this.

The methods of nursing the sick adopted in the public hospitals of Europe may be distinguished under five classes :—

1. Where the nurses belong to a religious order, and are under their own spiritual head; the hospital being administered by a separate and secular governing body.

Examples.—The hospitals of Paris, of King's College Hospital, London.

2. Where the nurses are of a religious order, the head of which administers both order and hospital.

Examples.—The Protestant institutions of Bethanien at Berlin, Kaiserswerth on the Rhine, many Roman Catholic institutions at Rome and all over Europe, also Anglican sisterhoods at home.

3. Where the nurses are secular under their own head; the hospital having its own separate and secular government.

Example.—The hospitals of London.

4. Where the nurses are secular; and under the same secular authority as that by which the hospital where they nurse is governed.

Examples.—The great general hospital at Vienna, the Charité at Berlin.

5. Where the nurses are all men and seculars, and under the same secular male authority as the hospital.

Example.—The military hospitals of Germany, and till a recent period of England,* France, and Russia.

* With regard to English army hospitals, this odious system of autocracy is done away with in a two-fold sense, both in regimental hospitals where female nursing is not (and cannot

Of these systems of nursing—

No. 1, where the nurses belong to a religious order, and are under their own spiritual head—the hospital being administered by a separate and secular governing body—is, on the whole, best calculated to secure good nursing for the sick, and the general well-being of both patients and nurses.

Of the great hospitals of Paris, four, Hôtel Dieu, St. Louis, Lariboisière, and La Charité, are nursed by the Augustinians; four, La Pitié, Beaujon, St. Antoine, and Cochin, by the Sœurs de Ste. Marthe; one, Necker, by the Sœurs de St. Vincent de Paul; two for children are nursed, one, Les Enfans, by the Sœurs de St. Thomas de Villeneuve; one, Ste. Eugénie, by the Sœurs de St. Vincent de Paul. The administration of all these, it is needless to say, is in the hands of secular men, the Assistance Publique. Great have been the 'scrimmages' from time to time between the administration and the orders; and great have been the benefits accruing to the sick from such 'scrimmages.' A testimony which will probably be considered fairer than mine, and which certainly would err on the side of the orders, if at all, has spoken out so much more strongly than I could venture to do, that I cannot forbear quoting him. La Rochefoucauld-Liancourt says, in his seventh Report, p. 3, "We cannot but believe that it is principally to the power exercised by the nuns in the Hôtel Dieu, and to their resistance to all authority, that the perpetuity of many abuses must be attributed, and of very great evils, of which we do not hesitate to denounce here the grievous effects." This was in 1790. Now the balance is most happily esta-

---

be) introduced, and in general hospitals where it is. Thus:—In regimental hospitals, the hospital buildings, furniture, diets, and all supplies required for the sick, except medicines, together with the washing, are in the hands of the purveyor, who is responsible to the War Office. The regiment stands in the relation of temporary tenant of the hospital. It brings with it its specially trained hospital sergeant and its specially trained orderlies, who, as long as they are competent, are attached solely to the service of the sick, and cannot be called on for any regimental duty. The nursing must be done to the satisfaction of the medical officer, who again is responsible to his commanding officer and to the Director-general of the Army Medical Department. For everything, then, connected with the building, lodging, and dieting of the sick, the purveyor is directly responsible—he being responsible, as above said, not to the commanding or medical officer, but to the Secretary of State for War, through the purveyor-in-chief. The purveyor supplies everything according to a fixed scale to prevent disputes, which scale, fixed after much consideration, is most liberal. And the regiment is responsible for the loss or breakage of all articles thus issued by the purveyor for its use.

In general hospitals, the governor, who is specially commissioned by the War Office, is responsible for everything, except for female nursing and medical treatment. All officers of the hospital are his officers, and are under him, not only as regards military discipline, but as regards the due performance of their special duties. The governor has, by regulation, power to provide all manner of supplies and furniture through the proper officer, who is his purveyor or steward. He has jurisdiction over all orderlies through the captain of orderlies, and is responsible for their discipline and their care in nursing the sick. He can suspend medical officers or female nurses. But the medical officer is responsible for the performance of his duties solely to the director-general; as are the nurses to the superintendent-general of nurses. No extraneous military authority has any jurisdiction within the walls of the hospital.

blished. The administration complains of the sisters, and the doctors wish the sisters "were completely under them." The sisters complain of the administration, and wish that the order "had it completely under itself." And all are the best possible friends, and the collision and competition does the greatest possible good. And all work much better for it, and none know how much evil it prevents, how much good it secures.

But in giving this unqualified opinion in favour of nursing by sisterhoods, *provided* the administration be secular, I must add a caution against two mistakes, whether committed in France or in England, in Roman Catholic or in Protestant institutions, viz. (1.) the female head of the sisters *must* reside in the institution nursed by them, and neither in a "nurses' home," or "Maison Mère," *not* the hospital, nor in a "home" where other works of charity, not hospital ones, are carried on. If she has other works of charity which appear to her more important, then she had better not undertake hospital ones. Hospital nursing is jealous, and demands her whole heart. It will not have a divided allegiance. It will not be too much of her whole life to gather experience and learn to govern such institutions. If she has several hospitals, as the Augustinians of Paris, the female head must live where the novices, or probationers, or whatever they are called, are trained. She must be at once matron of the hospital, which means of the nursing in it, and superintendent of the nurses. It will not do for her to head the nurses or probationers in their "home," and to leave the heading of them in the hospital to a matron, or other superior.

(2.) The sisters must not be the heads of wards merely in order to use 'moral influence,' as the inexperienced sometimes fancy will be sufficient. If a lady has, in addition, the same knowledge and experience as an old-fashioned hospital head nurse, which indeed many nuns, but only in secularly governed hospitals, have, good; she is fit to be sister or head nurse; if not, not.

No. 3, where the nurses are secular under their own secular female head, the hospital having its own separate and secular government—is, unquestionably, the system which secures the best nursing, after No. 1.

Out of the other systems of nursing, Nos. 2, 4, and 5, in each of which there is but one sole authority, although in No. 2 a religious one, in Nos. 4 and 5 a secular one, over both nurses and administration, are equally to be deprecated—

Nos. 4 and 5, because the nurses, whether male or female, are under the sole command of the male hospital authorities; in this case the arrangements as to hours, proprieties, and sanitary rules generally, would strike any one as all but crazy. Such are the rules which give nurses twenty-four hours "on duty" in a ward—or which put them to sleep with the sick, of which the extreme case is, where a female nurse is made to sleep in a man's ward, &c. &c. &c.

In No. 2, on the contrary, the nursing staff, whether Protestant or Roman Catholic, whether its heads be male or female, or both, is in entire and sole command of the hospital; in this case the arrangements are generally nearly as crazy as in the former, although the objects and results are widely different. Such are the letting a patient die of a bed-sore, because the nurse may spread the dressing for it, but must not look at it; the leaving the wards at night, or at times when the "community" assembles, in sole charge of subordinates, &c. &c. &c.

In Case No. 4 the nurses are destroyed bodily and morally, but the patients are generally, not always, better nursed.

In Case No. 2 the patients are not always, but generally, worse nursed; the sick are less cared for, while the spiritual good of the nurses is consulted. But the care of the sick is the object of hospitals.

The collision, often disagreeable, but generally salutary for the care of the sick, between the secular administration and the nursing staff (whether this consist of nuns, brothers, deaconesses, or nurses), as is the case in the hospitals of London and Paris, keeps each belligerent party to his duty, and reacts beneficially on the interests of the sick. Even the mutual impertinence, just as often to be heard between nuns and doctors, as between doctors and nurses, is far better for the management of a hospital, and any neglect of the sick is far less likely to pass unnoticed, than where the authority is solely invested in one of the two ways above mentioned; *i. e.*, either vested in the secular male authorities of the hospital, as is the case in the great general hospitals of Germany, or in the spiritual head of the nursing establishment, as is the case in German hospitals, nursed by either Protestant or Roman Catholic orders. Take the nuns, brothers, deaconesses out of the parent institution, and set them to work in a great secular hospital, in daily contact with the (often vexatious) exigencies of doctors and governors, and they will work admirably.

Take Case 2. Theory differs widely from practice in these things. If we were perfect, no doubt an absolute hierarchy would be the best kind of government for all institutions. But, in our imperfect state of conscience and enlightenment, publicity, and the collision resulting from publicity, are the best guardians of the interests of the sick. . A patient is much better cared for in an institution where there is the perpetual rub between doctors and nurses or nuns, between students, matrons, governors, treasurers, and casual visitors, between secular and spiritual authorities (for this applies quite as much to Roman Catholic as to Protestant institutions) than in a hospital under the best governed order in existence, where the chief of that order, be it male or female, is also sole chief of the hospital.

Taking the imperfect general run of human things, for we are considering men, and not angels, public opinion is a higher average standard than individual opinion. For many years I have been trying to find out how this could be, since public opinion is made up of individual opinions. I think it is because A will be much more rigid in making B mind B's business than in minding his own. Public opinion is good for this. The remark is not a high-minded one, but it is true.

Orders, whether Roman Catholic or Protestant, unless held in check by the rude curb of public opinion, or by the perpetual rub and collision with the secular authority of the hospital, are inclined to make into a special object the spiritual (often fancied) good of their members, and not the general and real good of the inmates of the hospital (for whom, nevertheless, the hospital was intended, and not for working out the salvation of the order).

It is bad for the activity of any one to have always his own way. And if it were only for this, viz., that no great sanitary or administrative improvements have ever come out of orders, or out of seculars, whose authority is undivided, it would be enough to condemn them.

Nos. 2 and 4. Where the nurses, religious or secular, are governed by the same authority, religious or secular, which governs the hospital, the destruction of health of the members both of orders and secular institutions often takes place in a period of about five years. This consumption of human beings is the worst policy in every sense. Its operative causes are—under-feeding, want of proper sleep, want of the most ordinary sanitary precautions—the result of austerity in orders, of an ignorant economy in secular institutions. In the latter, want of the most ordinary means for propriety and morality is often a fourth cause.

No. 2. In some institutions nursed by brotherhoods, abroad, a good Augustinian nun, or good hospital nurse from London, would turn everything out of window (though the former could not do all she would wish), and be as disgusted as we are with their pestilential filth. But, alas! this has been seen even in those nursing *sisterhoods* where the salutary check of the secular administration was not.

No. 2. Where institution and sisterhood alike are under the same authority. The following remark applies exclusively to orders, and to orders where no secular authority is in play, but much more to Protestant than to Roman Catholic orders, which latter have better sense:—

There is a constant change of occupation of each member of the order, for the sake of detaching said member from earthly things. To-day he or she is in the kitchen, to-morrow in a surgical ward, next week in a medical ward, the week after in the laundry. The perplexed medical attendant, when giving his directions about the patients, sees a new face, at least every fortnight, to give his directions to.

In the best Roman Catholic orders, especially where, as in 1, the secular authority comes into action, there is far more latitude given to individual character, and scope to individual capacity, than we are at all aware of. Each member is much more independent in his or her own occupation than is the case under arrangement No. 2.

Nos. 2, 4, and 5. Where there is but one authority over both hospital and nurses, whether that authority be religious or secular. The following remark applies alike to some institutions, both religious and secular, to all military, and to some civil, to Protestant and Roman Catholic establishments:—

The want of one definite head in permanent charge of each ward, or set of wards, invariably acts disastrously for the patients. There should always be some one person in acknowledged responsibility for the nursing, with servants—call them lay sisters or brothers, or assistant nurses, or what you will—under the head.

Religious motives, in some orders, a want of any practical system of nursing in many military and some civil hospitals, reproduce the above defect, in the most varied forms, in institutions of the most opposite character.

No. 4. Where nurses and institution are under the same secular authority. The following remark applies solely to institutions secularly nursed:—

The practice of having man and wife in joint-charge of a ward or wards has in it more evil than good for the patients. It is true that a woman had better flirt with her husband than with a student or patient; it is true that the common phrase "settling" (which means marrying in some classes) has its signification here—for some women never are "settled" till they are married. But it is no less true that the interest of the husband henceforth comes before that of the patients, in honest as in dishonest ways. The woman is no longer attached to her ward, but to her husband; and the patients are, more or less, neglected. This is still more eminently the case in regimental hospitals, where it is a common practice to choose married hospital sergeants, as being more "respectable," and to have the wife to live in the hospital. As well might the hospital head nurse have her husband to live with her in the room off her ward.

Nos. 1. Where the sisters are of a religious order, but the nurses are secular,—3 and 4. Where all the nurses are secular, whether governed by a separate head from that which governs the hospital, or by the same head:—The cardinal sin of paid nurses, of all classes, of all nations, is taking petty bribes and making petty advantages (of many different sorts and sizes) out of the patients. From this sin all orders, whether Roman Catholic or Protestant, are exempt; but from it their servants are by no means exempt.

The rules of hospital head-nurses in London, were they really religious women, who would neither take any present themselves, nor be guilty of any kind of impropriety, would enable them to exercise a far more efficient surveillance over assistant-nurses, as to both these things, than can be exercised by Roman Catholic or Protestant orders living in community. All kinds of things between nurses and patients may and do go on in the sisters' wards, when the sisters are out of the way. A hospital head-nurse is (or ought to be) always in command of her ward.

To sum up.—Case 1. There is a higher average care of the sick and a higher universal sense of morality, among hospital sisters, Protestant and Roman Catholic, provided the hospital authority be a secular one. Case 2. There is a lower average care of the sick, although an equally high morality, among hospital nuns, Protestant and Roman Catholic, if the hospital authority be not a secular one. Case 3. There is a far greater average care of the sick, although a lower morality, among nurses under a secular female head, the authority of the hospital being a secular and separate one, than in Case 2; and there is a somewhat higher average care of the sick in Case 4 than in Case 2, and no morality at all, but an awful destruction of both life and soul, among nurses, where both nurses and hospital are under the same secular (male) authority. Case 5. There is no care of the sick and no morality, nor even discipline, in hospitals where the nurses are men, and where both nurses and hospital are under the same secular (male) authority. This is the worst state of things of all. Case 2 is perhaps the second worst. For, take it which way you will, the idea of the "religious order" is always, more or less, to prepare the sick for death; of the secular, to restore them for life. And their nursing will be accordingly. There will be instances of physical neglect (though generally unintentional) on the part of the former; of moral neglect on that of the latter. Unite the two, and there will be fewer of either.

Of course to all this there are exceptions. This Appendix is dealing only with systems of nursing *as systems*.

NOTE.—Two excessively foolish books by the same woman, calling herself an "English Sister of Mercy," on this question of sisterhoods,—in which the difficulty is, not to find what is false, but to find what is true, and which I should never have thought of referring to, but that she has been quoted by grave divines in Consistory,—give every reason for the comparative usefulness or uselessness of sisterhoods but the right one, viz., that if a sisterhood cordially and frankly co-operates with and works in a secular institution, it is useful; if not, not.

NOTES ON HOSPITALS
Third Edition, 1863
BY FLORENCE NIGHTINGALE

The original book belongs to Professor Hiroyoshi Kobayashi, MD. PhD.

Reprinted 2006 by
SAIWAISHOBO Co. Ltd.
3-17, Jinbo-cho, Kanda,
Chiyoda-ku, Tokyo, JAPAN, 101-0051

NOTES ON HOSPITALS Third Edition, 1863
BY FLORENCE NIGHTINGALE
【復刻版】

2006年5月20日 発行

原本所蔵 小林寛伊

発行者 桑野知章
発行所 株式会社 幸 書 房
〒101-0051 東京都千代田区神田神保町3-17
TEL 03-3512-0165 FAX 03-3512-0166

印刷所／平 文 社
製本所／島崎製本

ISBN 4-7821-0265-8 C3047